BRADFORD
WASHBURN

An Extraordinary Life

BRADFORD
WASHBURN

An Extraordinary Life

BRADFORD WASHBURN

with

LEW FREEDMAN

WESTWINDS
PRESS®

Library of Congress Cataloging-in-Publication Data

Washburn, Bradford, 1910-2007.
  Bradford Washburn : an extraordinary life / Bradford Washburn and Lew Freedman.
    p. cm.
  Includes bibliographical references and index.
  ISBN 978-0-88240-907-8 (pbk.)
  1. Washburn, Bradford, 1910-2007. 2. Mountaineers—United States—Biography. 3. Photographers—United States—Biography. 4. Natural history museum directors—Massachusetts—Boston—Biography. I. Freedman, Lew. II. Title.
  GV199.92.W35A3 2013
  796.522092—dc23
  [B]
                    2013004999

WestWinds Press®
An imprint of Turner Publishing Company
www.turnerbookstore.com

Editor: David Abel
Design: Barbara Ziller-Caritey

For Barbara,
beloved companion for sixty-four years

B. W.

CONTENTS

Sherry and I hiked up 6,288-foot Mount Washington during the summer of 1925. I was fifteen; Sherry was thirteen and a half. It wasn't the first time for me, and certainly wasn't the last. I still have a special love for that mountain.

CHAPTER ONE

MOUNTAIN BEGINNINGS

On the morning after my first great mountain climb, I woke early on the summit of Mount Washington in New Hampshire to see the sun rise over the Atlantic Ocean. It was a sight that I will never forget. You almost never can distinguish the ocean in the view from the top of Mount Washington, because it meets the sky as a continuous blue horizon. The exception is very early in the morning on a clear day, when the sun is glittering off the water; that reflecting light is the ocean. The year of the climb was 1921 and I was eleven years old.

For most of my adult life, I have been associated with Mount McKinley in Alaska, as a climber, explorer, photographer, cartographer, and scientist. At 20,320 feet, McKinley is the tallest mountain in North America. Few people know of my love and nearly lifelong association with the much smaller Mount Washington, at 6,288 feet the tallest mountain in New England.

Mount Washington, the king of the White Mountains, provided my mountaineering start in a low-key way. My cousin Sherman Hall, from Portland, Oregon (and a student at Yale at the time), invited me along for the climb. As a youngster, I had terrible hay fever: awful sneezing fits and trouble breathing. July was the worst time. My nose would plug up and my eyes would tear. It was just awful. My family had decided on a new place for a summer vacation—Rockywold Camp on Squam Lake in New Hampshire—and Sherman joined us for a visit.

I knew nothing about Mount Washington. (I had previously hiked up a 1,200-foot hill called West Rattlesnake, which had a big rounded ledge and I've always said that for the amount of energy put in to get there that was the best view in the world.) Sherman and I climbed up the famous Tuckerman Ravine Trail, spent the night in the Summit House at the top, and rose early. We were rewarded with that terrific sunrise and distant view of the ocean.

The climb was scrambling all of the way. This was not a technical climb like my true climbing beginnings later in the French Alps. We simply put one foot in front of the other on the trail, and hauled ourselves up over the boulders. It was fun; and I quickly realized that the higher I climbed, the less my terrible hay fever bothered me. Eliminating my hay fever actually played a very important role in my future as a mountaineer: the higher I got above sea level, the better I felt. Finding a place where I didn't have hay fever was a real thrill.

We climbed in the summer, so the weather was mild, but one of the fascinating things about Mount Washington—and few world-class mountaineers ever give it a thought—is its fearsome reputation for extreme weather. The highest wind velocity ever recorded was taken at the observatory atop Mount Washington: 231 mph.

If you put an observatory on Mount McKinley, you would probably record higher velocities than the Mount Washington record. But I've always thought that there was something unusual about Mount Washington. It is shaped as a sort of dome, and if you went a thousand feet above the summit, there would not be as much wind as you get on top. I think the wind is squeezed up as it comes over the top, and there's more wind down on the lee side. You don't want to go fiddling around there in an airplane; it's terribly rough on the lee side.

My interest in Mount Washington grew from that little climb with Sherm Hall. In midsummer of 1925, I climbed it again with two schoolmates. We climbed the Webster Cliff Trail and then the Southern Peaks Trail, and spent the night at the Lake of the Clouds hut. The next day we went the whole way over the northern peaks of the Presidential Range, and my parents picked me up in their auto two days later at Randolph, New Hampshire.

My brother and I were adventuresome boys from the start. Here we're climbing our first mountain together in the winter of 1914, outside our home at 18 Highland Street, Cambridge, Massachusetts.

My mother took this picture in August 1925, as our little party was heading up the trail in the White Mountains. From left, Johnny LaFarge, Hunty Thom, me (at fifteen), and Hal Kellogg.

Then I returned to Mount Washington in the winter of that year for a Christmas climb with my father. We spent the night at the Glen House, and then walked up the road that runs to the summit, and then back down. That's sixteen miles up and back on that road in winter. I know that Mount Washington auto road very well. We used to call it the Carriage Road; in the old days, that was what it was used for—horse-drawn carriages.

It was moderately cold that day; the temperature was probably in the teens. It couldn't have been too windy or we wouldn't have made it all the way. We wore heavy wool trousers, wool long underwear, and heavy flannel shirts. We didn't have parkas in those days, just a windbreaker of sorts as a top layer. If it got too cold for that, you just didn't start. We wore the equivalent of hunting shoes on our feet, with rubber bottoms and leather tops. We also wore several pairs of woolen socks, which were pretty darned warm.

Mount Washington can be deadly. More than a hundred climbers have died on the mountain; they keep the list of deaths at the top, names of climbers and how they died. I think there are so many deaths on Mount Washington because it's so easy to get to—too many casual hikers take it for granted. There are bumper stickers that say, "This car climbed Mount Washington." That may fool some people into thinking it's an easy mountain to climb, but it can be an absolute son of a bitch if it wants to be, too.

After my first Mount Washington climbs, I climbed fairly often in the White Mountains, and later, when I got into map-making, I made a map of the Presidential Range. Sometimes my brother, Sherry, came along, or I went with local kids. I went up mountains fairly frequently in the summer. One reason to go out often was so I could breathe; I didn't have hay fever when I got a few thousand feet above sea level, and, of course, I didn't have it in the winter. Winter weather has never really bothered me.

Once I was climbing Mount Chocorua, also in New Hampshire, in the winter. It was Christmastime, and my brother and other friends were there and I said, "Let's try it." We got just below the top after a heavy, freezing rain and all of the rocks were veneered with ice. As we neared the top, I said,

In an early display of leadership, I organized the building of a tiny "hotel" atop 2,100-foot Mount Morgan, the highest summit of the Squam Range. It lies above Rockywold Camp, where my family stayed during the summers of the 1920s.

"I don't think that we should go any farther. I think this is as far as we can go and do this safely." My father was pleased; he thought I displayed good judgment and was not afflicted by summit fever. He said, "Once I saw that you knew to turn back, I was never worried about you on any mountain."

I was always a careful climber; I was never a daredevil. Later, when we were climbing in Alaska, we climbed with a purpose. It was not to show off or set records—there was almost always some science involved (like mapmaking), and we were not in a hurry.

By the time I was eighteen I had already written a book for boys about Mount Washington. It was called *Bradford on Mount Washington*, published by G. P. Putnam's Sons in 1928. It was part of Putnam's series of books written by boys, to be read by boys. As part of the preface I wrote, "In winter, during the months between December and April, it seems as though the slopes of Mount Washington were transported to Switzerland. Wild gales sweep the upper ridges of the mountain and its neighboring peaks. Terrific snowstorms fill the ravines to depths of over 100 feet." I made it sound like a pretty scary place. But I also wrote, "The view from Mount Washington is unsurpassed in all the East."

I have climbed Mount Washington a great many times. It was accessible via a short drive from the Boston area, and I always kept returning. I haven't kept track of exactly how many times I've climbed the mountain, but it was scores of times. And even now, when I am too old to climb it anymore, I keep in touch. I know the phone number for the observatory and call it regularly. Today when I called—it is January 27—it was 11 degrees, with 85 mph winds. It would not be a good day to try to climb Mount Washington.

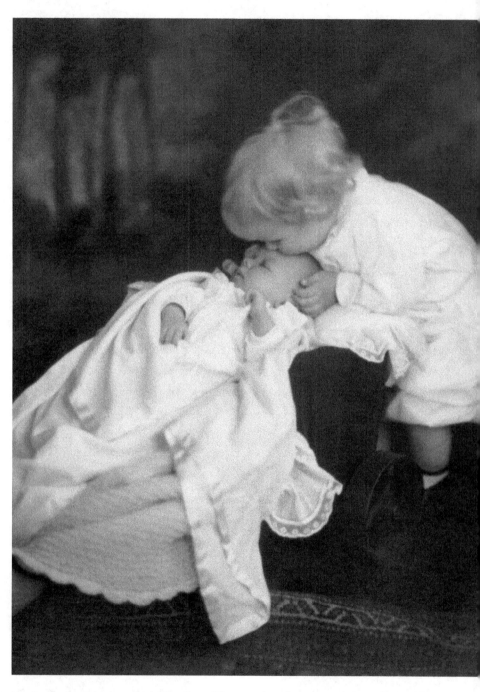

I got a first peek at my baby brother, Sherry, when he was only two days old.

CHAPTER TWO

EARLY DAYS AND FAMILY LIFE

I was born Henry Bradford Washburn, Jr., on June 7, 1910, at New England Baptist Hospital in Boston, Massachusetts. At that very time, the famous Sourdough Expedition was making its way to the lower summit of Mount McKinley, where the climbers erected a tall pole that they expected might be seen from Fairbanks, more than one hundred miles away. It was not visible, however. Of course, they thought they were climbing to the true summit, but they merely reached the top of McKinley's North Peak, 850 feet below the South Peak.

During most of my childhood, my family lived in Cambridge, across the Charles River from Boston. My father, Henry, was born in 1869 in Worcester, about thirty-five miles west of Boston, one of a family of six boys and one girl. He lived to be ninety-two, and for twenty years served as dean of the Episcopal Theological School of Cambridge.

My mother, Edith Buckingham Hall Washburn, was born in 1871 in Buffalo, New York, and was one of a family of six girls and four boys. She died at Rockywold Camp on Squam Lake—where we were staying when I first climbed Mount Washington—in 1952. She was married once before meeting my father, to Reverend Samuel Colgate. They were married in

1894, and he died of typhoid fever in 1902. She married my father in 1908.

As a result of my mother's first marriage, I had an older half sister, Mabel Hall Colgate, who lived to be eighty-nine, dying in 1984. My brother, Sherwood Larned Washburn, whom we called Sherry, was a very distinguished physical anthropologist who lived in Berkeley, California. He was a year and a half younger than I, and died in April of 2000 at the age of eight-eight. Longevity runs in my family.

I was perhaps a month old in this photo with my mother, taken at Onteora in the Catskill Mountains.

A few years ago, my wife, Barbara, had to have a minor operation on her back, and the surgery was scheduled at the Baptist Hospital. We were discussing things with the woman in the admitting office when she asked if we had any previous experience with that hospital. I said, "Yes, I have." Barbara turned to me and said, "What on earth is that about?" And I said, "On the seventh of June, 1910, at eight o'clock in the morning, I was born here!"

Previous generations of my family came from Harrison, Maine, which today is about a two-and-a-half-hour ride by car north of Boston. My grandfather made barbed wire and he made a bucket of money selling thousands of miles of barbed wire to the western ranges. This was my father's father, Charles Francis Washburn, but my father was named after his uncle, my grandfather's brother, Henry Bradford Washburn. Apparently there was a serious fire in the wire mill, and this young fellow lost his life from injuries sustained then. As he was dying, he said, "I hope if you ever have another son, you will give him my name." And that's how my father was named Henry Bradford Washburn. Actually, we can trace family members back to the *Mayflower*, although William Bradford is mentioned on the family tree (something like nine steps removed), he is not the chief connection. That was John Alden.

My mother first married into the famous Colgate family of New York, who had made a fortune selling toothpaste and all sorts of toiletries. My mother actually knew my father when she was still married to her first husband; both she and my father were in Germany at the same time, studying church history. People kidded my mother because she married the Colgate brother who went into religious work and didn't have any money.

My uncle Charlie, my father's oldest brother, made all of the big money in that family, in the wire goods business. He would give Sherry and me each a ten-dollar bill for Christmas. That would be something like a gift of 125 bucks today.

I had a wonderful relationship with my half sister, Mabel. She was fifteen years older than I, but we were always close, and she was always generous with us. She had a lot of the Colgate money, and she often gave Sherry and me nice presents. Everybody loved Mabel Colgate.

My mother's side of the family had connections to the Catskill Mountains in New York. They had a place in Onteora, which is about a hundred miles north of New York City. We made summer trips there when I was young, before we made the switch to the Squam Lake area of New Hampshire.

When I think back to my early life, that's what I remember best, the family getting together for vacations. My uncle, Gilbert Colgate, made his own big, private lake by damming up a rushing stream, and that's where I learned to swim. Mabel taught me. She put a piece of clothesline around my chest and tied a knot in it, then tied a stick about a yard long on the other end and walked along Uncle Gilbert's dam, holding me up. As I stroked in the water, she told me what to do. It took me no time to learn. She treated me as if I were a fish on a rod. When she said, "You're swimming," I hadn't realized I was doing it, and that she was no longer holding me up. Eventually, I won a diving contest at Squam Lake.

When I was six, my father had a major operation on his colon. Today, he would have that operation on a Monday and be out and walking in forty-eight hours. With the state of medicine in those days, he had a ten-inch scar all the way across his belly. Today he would be back to work in ten days or two weeks; they suggested he have a full year of rest before going back to work!

So we went all the way to California by train, and stopped at the Grand Canyon. I remember that my sister went down the

canyon on a mule and I walked a little bit down the Bright
Angel Trail to see what it looked like. Little did I realize I would
end up mapping the whole Grand Canyon for the National
Geographic Society during the 1970s! I remember little about
California, other than the wonderful weather. We stayed at a
place called the San Ysidro Ranch, and you could look down at
the ocean. Occasionally, we had picnic lunches at the beaches.

Sherry and I were dressed in our finest for this photograph at Onteora. I'm on
the left, and about four years old.

At the end of World War I, in 1917–18, we lived in New York City. Dad was the secretary of the War Commission of the Episcopal Church, which was sending chaplains to Europe to be with our fighting men. We were living at 76th Street, and one day my father called my mother and told her to bring my brother, Sherry, and me down to Wall Street as quickly as possible. The war was over and it was Armistice Day. There was a ticker-tape parade and it was fantastic.

My fifth-grade teacher, Florence Leatherby, at Cambridge's Buckingham School, had an enormous influence on me. She showed us maps of the world. She had a Hammond Atlas and it showed where gold was found, and copper, and coal. Looking at it, you had the feeling of the world being a live place instead of just a map. It gave me my interest in geography, and it excited me about the world and travel. I made my first map of Squam Lake in 1924, when I was fourteen.

I ended up attending the Groton School, a private high school in Groton, Massachusetts. It is very expensive, but my uncle Charlie paid the bill. The great majority of the students came from New York, and there were only a few of us who didn't come from wealthy families. We lived in dormitories on the campus and got an absolutely superb education.

Uncle Charlie was always generous to everyone in the family. He made that money in the wire business, and he was also a top official in the church. He actually died while making a speech to the Episcopalians of Massachusetts—he just plain died during the speech. He was the first dead person I ever saw. I was nearing the end of my schooling at Groton at the time.

Groton encouraged us all to work on special projects. I got interested in stained glass through a friend, and I made a long series of stained glass windows (in memory of a dear friend, Cleveland Arthur Dunn, who had died after a brief illness) that are still in place at the school. I put the coats of arms of Harvard, Yale, and other colleges into the windows. My brother also went to Groton, and he was a brilliant student. He always got marks in the 90s, whereas I scored in the 80s.

When we were kids we did not spend a lot of time together. That year-and-a-half age difference meant that we had our own groups of friends. We were friends as brothers, but we hung out with different groups of friends.

I was always close to my father and mother—I've always said that if you were to ask for a perfect set of parents, we came as close to it as you could possibly get. I saved a letter my father wrote to me during my early days at Groton, dated March 9, 1924, and it speaks about our relationship. He wrote, "Dear Braddy, the first marks look good to me. When things are easy take a little time for some of the things that are hard in spots. Keep everything cleaned up every day. Then you will be a happy man. We love you more than tongue can tell." And he signed it, "Always affectionately, Father."

My father was very practical. Both of my parents wanted Sherry and me to do what most interested us, but always to do it well. They were always pleased when we did well in school. Sherry pleased them a hell of a lot more than I did; he worked at it harder than I did. He was less involved in sports.

I was a pitcher on the Groton team that also had Charlie Devens, who went on to play for the New York Yankees for parts of three years in the 1930s. His strike ball would go by you so fast you wouldn't even realize it was in the catcher's glove. One day I was pitching for the Groton second team at Middlesex, and I was terrific that day. Just one strike after another. A kid came running across the diamond, put his hands up and pushed me off the pitcher's mound. What do you suppose he said? "Lindbergh's just been sighted off the coast of

My parents, Edith and the Reverend Henry Bradford Washburn, photographed in May 1932.

Ireland!" Charles Lindbergh landed in Paris later that night to complete the first transatlantic flight. (Later in life I would cross paths with Lindbergh in another way.) And then the game went on and we whipped the hell out of Middlesex.

I was also a quarterback on Groton's second football team, but I was not the starter. I was about 5' 8" and that was as tall as I ever got—I'm shrinking now. I don't remember what I weighed when I played football, but it wasn't very much. In 1951, when my team made the first ascent of Mount McKinley's West Buttress, I weighed about 154 pounds—all muscle. Now, in my nineties, I weigh 144, with very little muscle left.

In hockey, I was a wing. When I played baseball I batted right-handed, but in hockey I always shot left-handed.

I was never on a championship team, and I was not by any measure a great athlete. I was a good all-around athlete, but not a star at any one sport. I never ran track or long distances, but I had natural stamina that showed up in the mountains.

I wasn't one of those kids who want to be a cowboy or a fireman when they are seven years old. I didn't know what I wanted to be when I grew up. I knew I wanted to go to Harvard because my father and uncles went there. I graduated from Groton and entered Harvard as a freshman in 1929.

But by then I was already climbing mountains in Europe, and writing articles and books about my experiences in the Alps.

In the summer of 1926, when I was sixteen, my family traveled to the Alps, where I climbed Monte Rosa, the Matterhorn, and Mont Blanc, the highest peak in Europe. At 15,780 feet, it towers above the tiny village of Sallanches.

Chapter Three

CLIMBING IN THE ALPS

In the summer of 1926 my family took a trip to Europe. It was the journey that launched both my serious mountaineering career and my willingness and commitment to document my experiences so that others could learn from them.

At the age of sixteen, while visiting the Alps that summer, I climbed Mont Blanc (15,780 feet), Monte Rosa (15,217 feet), and the Matterhorn (14,690 feet).

My father had a semi-sabbatical that year, and he was in England for six months, beginning in January, studying church history. At the end of the school year my mother took Sherry and me across the Atlantic Ocean by boat; we left from Montreal. There was a debate over whether we should sail north or south of Newfoundland. They decided there were too many icebergs to the north and they didn't want to risk hitting one, so we took the southern route to Liverpool. We met my father there, and then we crossed the English Channel into France.

We took the train to Lyon and discovered that we could get airplane flights from Lyon to Geneva. These were ancient World War I biplanes. Sherry and mother flew with one pilot, and dad I flew with the other. As we came up over the foothills of the Alps and began the descent for our landing in Geneva,

Mont Blanc was towering over the landscape. It was by far the biggest mountain I had ever seen—so lofty, way above everything else. I'll never forget that sight.

We had supper in Geneva, rented a car, and drove through the hills for about sixty miles to Chamonix. As we neared the town, Mont Blanc rose above us, silhouetted in the moonlight. Then, sometimes as clearly as if it were daylight, the moon brightened the spires of the Aiguilles (the Needles) to the left of Mont Blanc. What a spellbinding drive! It was very impressive, but I already knew what to expect because of my reading.

The previous Christmas, an aunt and uncle had given me a book called *Mont Blanc*, by Roger Tissot, and for my sixteenth birthday (shortly before the trip), I had been given another mountaineering book called *Climbs on Alpine Peaks*, by Abate Achille Ratti (who later became Pope Pius XI). These two treasured books had a great influence on me. They inspired my

My parents at Squam Lake, New Hampshire, in 1932. Both of them encouraged us to do what we wanted, but to give it our all. They fed my love of mountaineering during that 1926 trip to the Alps, when I climbed three peaks in less than two weeks.

interest in climbing—and in mountain photography, as both of them were beautifully illustrated with wonderful photographs. I have kept these volumes close to my heart and as a cornerstone of my book collection for more than seventy-five years. To actually visit the Alps so soon after reading those little books was a thrilling opportunity, especially for a teenaged boy.

By then, of course, my interest in mountains was widely known to family members and family friends. I had not only climbed Mount Washington more than once, but had gone to other peaks in the White Mountains. In the summer of 1925, when my family was occupying a cottage called Platt 24 at Rockywold, Mrs. Armstrong (who then ran Rockywold) became so convinced that I would climb Mount Everest that she started calling one of the cottages "Everest." (Her prophecy was not quite correct. I never got a chance to attempt a climb of Everest, but much later I did spend years making the first detailed and definitive map of the Everest area.)

My fascination with Everest did not begin until a year after Mrs. Armstrong made her prediction. In the fall of 1926, Captain John Noel—a member of the 1924 Everest expedition on which George Mallory and Sandy Irvine were lost—gave a lecture at the Groton School. Noel had been the official expedition photographer, and he showed us superb movies and colored slides.

I was enthralled. At the time I was the managing editor of Groton's *Third Form Weekly* newspaper, and wrote a short piece about Noel's appearance. The last paragraph of my story read, "Captain Noel gave us a vivid picture of both the beauty and hardships of an Everest expedition, and we are indebted to him for a most enjoyable evening." The story appeared on October 9, 1926, only weeks after the return from my first climbing excursion to Europe.

So there I was in the Alps with my family at the beginning

of August. I hadn't made any plans, except that I wanted very much to climb Mont Blanc. I'd been told the ascent did not involve any technical difficulties and that guides could be obtained. The guides at Chamonix (the start of the route) required clients to make a couple of low, relatively easy ascents

---

I heard a story about Mount Blanc—a local legend, actually, but I think it is probably true. After Jacques Balmat and Michel Gabriel Paccard made the first ascent of Mont Blanc on August 8, 1776, Horace Benedict de Saussure, a very famous and wealthy scientist who lived in Geneva, tried to climb Mount Blanc repeatedly—but always failed. De Saussure at last hired Balmat as a guide.

In 1777, de Saussure put together a huge scientific party for an ascent of the great peak. They even brought ladders to facilitate the crossing of big crevasses. They carried a heavy mercurial barometer to calculate Mont Blanc's exact altitude, and brought along a tent to erect on the summit to make it much easier to carry out their work on top.

When, after the end of this "First Scientific Ascent of Mont Blanc," de Saussure returned to Geneva, he was greeted by an elderly woman, who observed that when Balmat and Paccard had made their climb, they had taken only a couple of days of food, some rope, and a lot of guts. Why did de Saussure need such a huge party, and such a mass of equipment?

De Saussure's reply was speedy and succinct: "Science is like a very wealthy woman who travels with a lot of luggage."

---

to prove their fitness. The first was a very long, steep hike above the valley; the second involved the ascent of the Aiguille de l'M, the top of which looked exactly like the letter M. I made both of these climbs easily. Then I was given an experienced guide called Alfred Balmat, and a porter called Georges Cachat. (I'm not aware of any relation between the two Balmats: Alfred and Jacques.)

The first part of the trail up Mont Blanc was very hot and dull. Each day it was used mostly by hundreds of tourists who wanted to see the view from the Chalet des Pyramides, about halfway to the tree line. There we had lunch, and I amused myself by looking through a very powerful telescope. I could see my brother, Sherry, walking back and forth outside our room in the Astoria hotel, thousands of feet below us. This also proved to be an excellent vantage point from which to see the big glacier on this slope of Mont Blanc, the Glacier des Bossons. There, all of us put on our yellow snow glasses to protect our eyes from the glare of the sun on the snow and ice cover, over which we now continued climbing.

This part of the climb is called the "junction," because it is the area where the two great glaciers on this side of Mont Blanc—the Glacier des Bossons and the Glacier de Taconnaz— separate for their descent into the valley. In this area, too, there are scores of crevasses and a dangerous jumble of ice.

For quite a distance the going was almost horizontal; then the slope suddenly steepened again in the late afternoon, as we neared the Grands Mulets hut where we planned to spend the night. Powerful professional packers, hauling tremendous loads, climbed each day to the hut to keep it well stocked with food and fuel. We reached the hut in late afternoon, exhausted from the seven-thousand-foot climb from Chamonix. We had an excellent dinner, with lots of wine and revelry, and went to bed at about ten.

The summit of the Aiguille Verte in Chamonix-Mont-Blanc after our first ascent of its north face on September 6, 1929. We did it in six hours and twenty minutes from the little cabane d'Argentière, where we'd spent the night. I'm standing at left, next to guide Alfred Adolphe Couttet and assistant guide Georges Charlet.

The wake-up call came all too soon, shortly after midnight. We ate a meager breakfast of cheese, tea, toast, and butter before setting out at about one in the morning. We now strapped on crampons for a better grip on the frozen snow surface, and for the next two hours we climbed by lantern light. Eventually, a small pink glow hinted at the arrival of dawn. To our right towered the breathtaking snow and ice face of Dome du Gouter.

Around 6:30 A.M., the sun became so strong, it seemed as if it was burning my eyes. Then I felt a twinge of sickness in my stomach, though my strength held up, even though I did not eat again until well into the descent. The guides said I had mountain sickness from lack of oxygen. Whenever we stopped to rest, I felt drowsy. The path we followed in the deep snow was narrow, only about eighteen inches wide, and the climb was really exhausting.

At about 10:00 A.M., we reached the snowy summit of Mont Blanc, and it was beautiful. The wind was calm (though it was extremely cold) and the view was stupendous. We could see the Zermatt Mountains, the huge bulk of Monte Rosa, the great spire of the Matterhorn, the Dolomites of Italy—and Lake Geneva way, way below us.

I was lucky that we could complete the trip so quickly. The snow conditions were very good, but it did take a lot of stamina. This was a big jump for me, going from Mount Washington to Mont Blanc. It was a thrilling experience to climb a world-renowned mountain, but it was not technically difficult at all. I just had to have the guts to keep putting one foot in front of the other. It's thirteen thousand feet up and thirteen thousand feet down in forty-eight hours. That's a lot of just plain hiking!

It was an exciting achievement, especially since I went on to climb Monte Rosa, and the Matterhorn in Switzerland, too, in a period of about two weeks. I had the same disagreeable midnight breakfasts on Monte Rosa and the Matterhorn. Oh for some good, old oatmeal, bacon, and eggs!

Awakened for a 1:00 A.M. departure for the Matterhorn from the Belvedere hut, I switched the menu to a cup of hot milk and three crackers. Within two hours I was climbing up the Matterhorn with my guide, Gottfried Perrin. Right out of the hut, we started climbing up thousands of feet of rotten, loose rock. There was no wonderful granite like at the peaks at Chamonix.

Although the final slope to the summit is often bare rock, it was snow-covered when I climbed it . . . very carefully. I was warned repeatedly to put my feet into my guide's steps. We reached the summit at 7:45 A.M. and it was a tiny snowdrift. It appeared flimsy, as if it might peel off and fall into Italy at any moment. In the distance, about sixty miles away, I could see Mont Blanc, so large in relation to the other nearby peaks that it looked like a great snowy cloud.

It was terrific that I had been able to climb both Mont Blanc and the Matterhorn, the same mountains that I had read about in my favorite books. Now I had seen them firsthand. I also took a large number of pictures.

I was carrying the same type of camera that Sandy Irvine had carried in 1924 when he disappeared on Mount Everest. It was a Kodak vest pocket autographic special that I got as a Christmas present. This model was made between 1921 and 1926. In 1925, it cost $21, which in 2004 dollars would be close to $250. It had two speeds, 1/25 and 1/50 of a second, and I always used the faster speed. Each roll of film produced six 2¼ x 3¼–inch pictures. The camera weighed only twelve ounces, which was especially advantageous for climbing.

In a way, this camera laid the foundation for my career of mountaineering, photography, mapmaking, and public science education. I used it to take the pictures that accompanied my *Youth's Companion* articles on Mont Blanc and the Matterhorn in 1927. These were my first published articles. I'd like to say I was motivated by other reasons to write them, but mostly I needed the money (even if I can't now remember how much they paid). The articles also led to my writing *Among the Alps with Bradford* later. George Putnam's son had written the first book in

Descending the Aiguille du Grand Dru, Chamonix, 1929. Leading, at left, is guide Georges Charlet, followed by David Murray, my brother, Sherry, and me.

I shot this image of the Vallot Refuge in 1931. At 14,375 feet, it's still 1,400 feet below the summit of Mont Blanc (15,770 feet). Joseph Vallot built the shelter in the late 1800s as an aid to climbers who were caught in storms at this great altitude, or for those suffering from "mal de montagne"!

his series for boys, called *David Goes to Greenland*. (I think that was a bigger seller than mine.) I considered it a heck of an idea to write a book because I was going to get paid. By then I had written a little guidebook, *Trails and Peaks of the Presidential Range of the White Mountains*, whose publication was financed by my uncle Charlie—actually, that predated the articles about climbing in Europe, and was my first substantial effort to share what I had learned in the mountains.

My book on the Alps was actually written a year later, in 1927, when my family returned to Europe for another vacation. The book was dedicated to our guides on that summer's climb, Alfred Couttet, Georges Charlet, and Antoine Ravanel. But what I remember most clearly about that summer was that my family had a marvelous time touring Venice after the climbs, while I had to stay indoors, writing my book, at a hotel called the Pensione Calcina.

Putnam had said, "I want to have that book either clearly written in handwriting or typewritten, and in my hand, by the 15th of September." I gave him the book in longhand on the 15th of September and it was on sale by the middle of November. (That doesn't happen with books today!)

When I look back, it seems extraordinary that I was a published author at the age of seventeen. When I got the first royalty check for *Among the Alps with Bradford*, I bought my first automobile: a Ford Roadster, with a rumble seat, that cost $520. I drove up to the White Mountains in it and had a marvelous time.

The book was a success and George Putnam was interested in having me write another. That's where the book *Bradford on Mount Washington* came in. He wanted to go up the mountain with me in the winter, so I took him along. When we got about a third of the way up, he said, "The hell with this. This isn't my thing." It was cold and miserable, and the snow was often loose and fluffy, and nearly waist deep.

I'm not sure if that left him more impressed with me or not, but he had little sense of humor about that, or anything else. George Putnam was a really nice, but hard-boiled guy.

My brother, Sherry, took this photo. By 1929, I had already been to the Alps three times, and my climbing boots showed it.

CHAPTER FOUR

LECTURE TOURS AND
A HARVARD EDUCATION

I graduated cum laude from the Groton School in the spring of 1929, and entered Harvard in the fall. Few people would guess my major at Harvard: French history and literature. Unofficially, you might say, I was minoring in mountains. By the time I enrolled at Harvard I had been back to the Alps for a third time, and had a growing interest in photography—and even motion pictures. I took the photographs that accompanied my *Youth's Companion* articles, but after the 1927 climbs I worked with professional photographer Georges Tairrez of Chamonix to produce a 16-millimeter film, *The Traverse of the Grands Charmoz and the Grepon.*

During the summer of 1929 I returned to the French Alps for two months with my family. Joining up again with guides Alfred Couttet and Georges Charlet, I participated in many first ascents in the mountains. My best Alpine climb to date was accomplished that season when we made the first ascent of the north face of the Aiguille Verte.

I then borrowed $500 to finance a 35-millimeter film, made with Georges Tairrez, this time called *The Traverse of the Grepon.* My mother had been the toughest critic of the first film: she suggested that my vest pocket camera was too small for my goals, and that I would be better off including people, as well as scenery, in my next film. I heeded her suggestions on both counts. For this project, I used a 4 x 6 Ica Trix German camera which provided large-format negatives for photographing large subjects, such as the wonderful views, along with the close-up pictures of us while we were actually climbing.

In 1928 and 1929, at roughly the same time that I was working on the stained glass windows at Groton, the school officials had let me have my own little photographic lab in the basement of the school's main building. That's when I really began working on my own.

For the moment—after high school, and into college—I was keeping myself in spending money by writing and lecturing. I traveled around showing pictures and giving talks about the Alps. In 1930 I met Burton Holmes, the famous travel lecturer. He bought my climbing movie, and suggested that I join him in the rounds of Carnegie Hall in New York, the Academy of Music in Philadelphia, Symphony Hall in Boston, and Orchestra Hall in Chicago. He said, "I want you to come around with me and show movies of your climbs as part of my lecture show."

That was a big break for me. It gave me a lot of experience in public speaking and working with him got me into a lot of places where I thought I might like to lecture on my own at some point. He also gave me advice that I never forgot and always use. He said, "If you're going to speak in a big hall don't ever look at the people right in front of you when you're on the stage. It's okay to peek at them once in a while, but I want you to talk to the first balcony, way back, because if you talk to the people in front of you, your voice won't go all the way back."

I can't remember how big the audiences were at these appearances—some a hundred or so, and others were a thousand. After I got into college, however, I started giving my talk on the Alps all over the place. I got a call from Mr. A. H. Handley, who ran a lecture agency in Boston. He became my agent, and during Christmas vacation he said, "If you give me a week, I'll make you a lot of money. We'll go out to the Chicago area."

I gave talks at clubs in some of the fancier communities along Lake Michigan. When I reported back to him that the people in one of my lecture halls were an awfully dull crowd to talk to, Handley responded, "The feeling was mutual!" Handley would ask members of the crowd, "How did you like it?" You could use the good comments to help get jobs somewhere else. It was clear that one or two of my audiences didn't like snow and ice at all.

When I began giving lectures I had no public speaking experience whatsoever. But I must have been reasonably good, otherwise they wouldn't have kept hiring me. I concentrated on the serious parts of climbing, but I also mixed in some jokes. And I did try to improve. I took a public speaking course at Harvard (for no credit), and I did learn about how to dress and how to talk to the audience. I had to deliver a speech once a week in the class, so that conquered any nervousness I still had.

Much worse, in my regular classes, I had to write a thousand-word composition, once a month, all of the way through Harvard. My senior year it was fifteen hundred words. We could pick any subject to write on, and I found it difficult to come up with topics. In those days I found it much easier to speak than to record my thoughts on paper.

Probably the most exciting audience I lectured to was the National Geographic Society—my first lecture for that famous organization, which I was later to be involved with so extensively. The lecture took place on March 28, 1930, at Constitution

Hall in Washington, D.C., and was titled "Treading a New Trail to Green Needle's Tip," the story of my first ascent of the North Face of the Aiguille Verte in 1929. I was still only nineteen years old, and spoke to an audience of more than a thousand people.

What I could not have foreseen after our third trip to Europe was a change in economic fortunes. When the stock market crashed in the fall of 1929, triggering the Great Depression, my family no longer had the funds to help me finance my excursions; I had to produce all of the money from my lectures.

By then I was at Harvard and had joined the school's mountaineering club. This meant that I met like-minded students who also had a passion for the mountains. I became lifelong friends with classmate Bob Bates, who in the coming years accompanied me on some terrific adventures in Alaska, and with whom I made many weekend climbs in the White Mountains while we were still in school. I also met Charlie Houston, who later made the first ascent of Alaska's huge Mount Foraker, and who, along with Bob, made the first significant American attempts to climb K-2 (the world's second-tallest mountain; in the Himalayas) in 1938 and 1953. Also, H. Adams Carter, of Milton, Massachusetts (later president of the American Alpine Club), became an excellent climbing companion and remained a lifelong friend after our Harvard days. I met a lot of interesting people through the Harvard Mountaineering Club; I guess you could say we all helped write chapters of American mountaineering history.

One thing that we young mountaineers did during our weekend trips to Mount Washington was to build the Harvard Cabin on the Tuckerman Ravine Trail. We also had a different type of thrill early in my stay at Harvard: we had a visit from

Noel Odell, the respected British mountaineer, who had been on the 1924 Everest expedition. Later Odell taught geology, and I enjoyed a few Christmas dinners with him. John Noel, whom I had heard at Groton, had been the official photographer for that expedition, but Odell was the last person to see George Mallory and Sandy Irvine alive before they disappeared into the clouds. Listening to him speak, and having him as a friend, excited me even more about the prospect of exploring more in the higher mountains, and of one day climbing Everest.

Some of the money I made from lecturing went toward paying off my education. But I also put money aside to spend on future expeditions.

In 1930, after hearing Allen Carpe lecture on his failed Fairweather climb in Alaska, I was filled with enthusiasm and optimism. I'd never been to Alaska before, but nonetheless, I gathered a group of guys to attempt the mountain. This photo shows the northeast face of the summit. The huge gathering grounds of snow feed the ice of Glacier Bay's Margerie Glacier.

Chapter Five

Welcome to Alaska

It has been seventy-four years since I made my first trip to Alaska. In 1930, I could not have imagined how important that vast territory would become to my life—and that I would go to Alaska more than seventy times!

I knew a man named Harry Pierce Nichols, then more than eighty years old, who had climbed Mount Washington at least once a year for decades—that was how we met. He was the principal minister of a church in New York, and he invited me to stay with him for a night and attend a presentation at the American Alpine Club.

The subject was Mount Fairweather in Alaska, and the lecturer was Allen Carpe, who had led an expedition attempting to make the first ascent in 1926. They didn't make it, and that was the story he told. Carpe was an accomplished mountaineer (who would die too young in a tragic accident in Alaska two years later), and his show intrigued me. I was young and strong and enthusiastic, and had climbed in the Alps. I knew nothing about Alaska except that they had once had a gold rush, but it sounded exciting.

When I heard that Carpe's group didn't make it to the top of Mount Fairweather, I said to myself, "Gee, here's an opportunity. I have climbing experience. I'll go out and try to do it." I got a bunch of guys together to go after it. Alaska seemed like the end of the world.

Fairweather was a huge, snow-covered mountain, with no obvious route to its top. I knew there weren't any Alpine huts and we would have to camp out. I knew there weren't any guides. It was a whole new ball game, an exciting opportunity. The adventure and novelty of it appealed to me.

Fairweather is located in Southeast Alaska, at 15,330 feet, the tallest mountain of the Fairweather Range—one of the tallest coastal mountain ranges in the world. The area is difficult to access and the mountain is surrounded by wilderness. A good friend, Bob Morgan, had been on the 1925 expedition that climbed Mount Logan, at 19,550 feet the tallest mountain in Canada, and second only to Mount McKinley as North America's tallest, and he helped me with the planning. (One thing we did was study a short article about Carpe's attempt.)

I got a six-man crew together (Bob couldn't come because business kept him in Boston) and at the age of twenty, I organized the first expedition of my career. Although I didn't know it then, this set a pattern. Except for some trips that I took during World War II that had military connections, I was the organizer of every expedition I took to Alaska.

At the time I never gave it a thought that I was the leader of an expedition at such a young age. I haven't the slightest idea what gave me the confidence to think I could do it. All I did was say to a few guys that it seemed like this could be an exciting trip. We then added a few more people, and the next thing I knew we were an expedition. I think I eventually developed a reputation as someone who is a meticulous and careful planner for mountain trips. But it was not true then. My friends and I had a lot to learn.

I fell in love with Alaska the first time I saw it. I absolutely loved it. Mount Fairweather is located just west of Glacier Bay. Past a sliver of Alaska, British Columbia stretches to the east and the Yukon Territory to the north. To the west is the Gulf of Alaska. Alaska's capital city of Juneau is the closest major community and is east of Glacier Bay, close to the Canadian border, about a hundred miles from Fairweather.

My old benefactor George Putnam eventually played a part in my Fairweather experience. He hired me to write another boys' book. Of course, by then, I was no longer a lad and didn't quite qualify, but we stretched it, and in 1930 the account of our trip, *Bradford on Mount Fairweather,* appeared in print. This was again a case in which a book made it into the stores only months after the expedition ended.

At least I knew a little bit more about Alaska by the time that I wrote the book. The opening of the book certainly implied it, anyway; I wrote, "Alaska! The word alone thrills us with the glamor of exploration and adventure. Thousands of miles of unexplored rivers, vast expanses of virgin forest, glaciers, gold mines, pack trains—all these flash through our minds at the very mention of that magic country." I also noted, "Out of the hundreds of beautiful peaks that still remain untouched by man, probably the most beautiful is Mount Fairweather."

Carpe's 1926 attempt had begun six miles north of Cape Fairweather at Sea Otter Bight. We planned to use the same landing spot, but the fellow who ran our boat refused to land there, saying there were too many rocks and reefs. We explored alternative landing areas, and bounced around in the rough waters trying to find a suitable starting point for our climb. In doing so we wasted considerable time, and knew that we would be climbing against the clock. The last boat of the season left Juneau on

August 30, and we had to be on it. Already the likelihood of making the ascent of Fairweather had become dubious.

Our inexperienced little party managed to reach an altitude of about 6,500 feet, then ran out of both food and fuel. So we quit after seemingly endless backpacking along Desolation Valley. We retreated to the mountain's base and did a reconnaissance of the area. I was not sure if we would ever return, but we thought to document our observations with the written word and with photographs.

In 1931, a year later, it was Allen Carpe who returned and, accompanied by Terris Moore (a man who later became one of my best friends), accomplished the first ascent of Fairweather. It was a great achievement. I learned of their climb from a French newspaper while I was in the Alps for yet another summer. (That year I finally returned to Mont Blanc, and Sherry climbed it with me.)

Carpe is pretty much forgotten in Alaska today, at least in public terms, because he did not have a very long career. He was a respected research engineer at Bell Laboratories who studied cosmic rays, and made trips to Alaska and the north whenever he could. He led the first ascent of Fairweather, and was involved in the first ascents of Mount Logan and 16,550-foot Mount Bona. His expedition to Mount McKinley in 1932 was one of only two to try to climb the mountain since Hudson Stuck's inaugural successful ascent in 1913.

Terry Moore—who later became the president of the University of Alaska Fairbanks, and who was my pilot on Mount McKinley in 1951—said that when he climbed Fairweather with Carpe in 1931, Carpe never roped up. You can't climb mountains like Fairweather and McKinley unroped without losing your life unless you're god-damned lucky. It's just foolishness. Carpe paid the price with his life on his 1932 McKinley

On the beach near Cape Fairweather, Alaska, with a ninety-pound pack, in August 1930. I was about to start the twelve-mile hike to Lituya Bay.

expedition, when he fell into a crevasse and disappeared. Later, a 12,550-foot mountain very near to Mount McKinley was named Mount Carpe in his honor.

I remember vividly Terry telling me that in 1931, when he, Carpe, Andy Taylor, and Bill Ladd were trying to climb Fairweather, they were running out of food and there was a great discussion about who wanted to go on and who wanted to quit. One of them said, "If we don't get to the top, that son of a bitch Washburn will do it next year. You just wait and watch." Bill Ladd and Andy Taylor descended, and Terry and Carpe made the ascent alone.

They were right about me coming back and trying to climb Fairweather. In 1932 I went back with a group, planning to make the second ascent of the mountain. I still thought we could do it. We flew into the area where we wanted to start and the lake we planned to land on was frozen solid. So we landed at Lituya Bay, far from the right spot, and I said to the other fellows, "Let's get together and try to climb Mount Crillon." Mount Crillon was a superb peak towering right above the bay, 12,728 feet high and unclimbed. You looked right at it. We had a wonderful group of eager, enthusiastic, young climbers who agreed, "The hell with Fairweather. Let's try to climb Crillon."

CHAPTER SIX

MOUNT CRILLON:
MY FIRST "FIRST" IN ALASKA

I was disappointed when Carpe made the first ascent of Mount Fairweather, but that didn't discourage me from going back. I learned from Fairweather and Crillon that Alaska's mountains were big and difficult and would take more experience and planning than I had.

As we approached Mount Crillon, we hiked over a ridge while carrying a canoe, because we didn't know what we were going to face. We brought the canoe to Crillon Lake, where it was a very valuable asset at base camp. This first trip to Crillon mostly proved how challenging the whole endeavor would be.

We were overconfident in the beginning, and frustrated by the end of the summer. The trip, which I called the Harvard Expedition (and which included my friend Bob Bates), turned out to be only an exploratory mission. We backpacked for three weeks to the base of the mountain, and realized that climbing Crillon might present as many obstacles and problems as climbing Fairweather.

The following year, when we approached Crillon for the second time—now calling ourselves the Harvard–Dartmouth Alaskan Expedition—we were under the impression from charts that Crillon Lake had been drained in the interim, that it no

The 1933 Mount Crillon team at our 6,000-foot camp. From left, Charlie Houston, Bob Bates, Bill Child, me, Walt Everett, and Ad Carter.

longer existed. We discovered not only that the lake was still a lake, but that it was a mile longer than had been shown on the maps. We used a seaplane to bring in one thousand pounds of gear and eliminate the need for the long overland approach march.

I had come to Crillon not only to be among the first to reach the summit as a mountaineer, but also to study the geology of the region and gain comprehension of the glaciers surrounding it. For the rest of my climbing career, mountaineering and scientific pursuits were almost always intertwined.

The use of the airplane made a huge difference for us: not only did it allow us to avoid carrying in all of the equipment, it enabled us to choose a more comfortable location for a base camp. Unlike modern climbers who, typically, come to an area, make a speedy ascent of a mountain, descend, and depart, we planned on making a season of our climb. We were not merely laying down camps to climb the peak, we were performing time-consuming scientific studies.

Richard Goldthwait of Dartmouth, assisted by Russell Dow and Howard Platts of New Hampshire, spent the entire summer on two projects. They studied the movements of the South Crillon Glacier, and conducted a geologic survey of the nearby mountains. We did not neglect the mountain itself, however. A climbing party of six twice attempted to ascend Crillon's slopes. A vicious winter-style storm turned us back the first time at 11,750 feet. The second time we reached the east summit at 12,390 feet before awful weather again forced us to retreat. We had no time for a third assault that summer. We were running out of food.

Before leaving the area, however, Goldthwait and I surveyed the glaciers of the region from a plane with pilot Gene Meyring. We recorded data and I was able to get marvelous photographs all the way up the coast as far as Yakutat. This

Writing in my diary in the big wall tent at our Crillon Lake base camp.

research provided the information we needed to establish a climbable route to the summit of Mount Crillon, as well as offering lasting expertise to help future visitors.

Without much premeditation, but drawn by the fantastic beauty and challenges of a virtually unknown (and, in many cases, unmapped) area, I had transferred my summer vacations from the Alps to Alaska. At the same time, I had been progressing toward my degree at Harvard. While there I organized the school's ski program (which later earned me a medal from the directors of the Harvard Athletic Association), became president of the Harvard Mountaineering Club, and was elected to membership in the American Alpine Club. After earning my undergraduate degree in 1933, I had immediately begun graduate study in surveying and aerial photography at Harvard's Institute of Geographical Exploration. One of my most influential instructors there was Captain Albert W. Stevens (who, in 1935, made the highest balloon flight in history, 72,395 feet, for the National Geographic Society).

But Crillon represented unfinished business, and my new studies and work at the Institute fitted naturally to geologic research and an ascent of the mountain. Goldthwait also had work there he wanted to finish. In 1934, we formed a second Harvard–Dartmouth Alaskan Expedition, using all of the knowledge we had gained in two previous visits to the peak to make our plans.

We committed to spending our whole summer vacation in Alaska. Now, climbers take a jet plane to Anchorage, get a ride to Talkeetna, fly on a small plane to the Kahiltna Glacier, and pretty much wrap up a climb of Mount McKinley in three weeks. We had no time limit, other than that we knew we had to be back in Massachusetts for school in the fall. We didn't have to worry about rushing back to our jobs, even though I had become assistant director of the Institute. This was geographical exploration, so it was part of my job.

Each year we learned more and became more competent. One innovation we brought to Crillon on the third trip was the use of very high frequency 56-megacycle radios for intercamp communications. This was the first time that mountaineers, in addition to using a larger radio at base camp to obtain weather reports or contact an airplane, had used these "walkie-talkies" to stay in touch between camps while climbing a high mountain anywhere.

We were also the first to air-drop supplies to high camps. I had become more and more intrigued by the growing possibilities of aviation in approaching high mountains. Before our arrival in Alaska I had made my first solo flight in a Kinner-Fleet biplane from Boeing Field in Seattle. It had taken us four days by train to get across the country, and we had to wait in Seattle for the boat to Alaska. I filled the waiting time well (and at the end of the summer I passed the flight exam for a private flying license at Roosevelt Field, on Long Island, in New York—No. 32,898).

On Crillon, the airplane was very helpful, and the radios were terrific. I also had a tremendous interest in radios. (My Alaska radio license was KXU2; decades later I had those letters and numbers on my Massachusetts automobile license plate.) On the mountain we had what were called five-meter sets. We could chat back and forth from the mountain to base camp at Crillon Lake. We communicated about where supplies were to be dropped, and helped pinpoint them so the men on the ground knew where to look.

The third trip to Crillon was the fourth Alaskan expedition I organized; and I was the team leader. I had not specifically set out to be a leader and an organizer, but whatever qualities and abilities I had in those areas had developed over time; and must

I took my first airplane flight at Revere Beach, which is right next to Boston, in June 1923. The family was at the beach, and it was my birthday. It cost $5 to take a flight, and my mother wanted to do it with me. She had the instinct for excitement; my dad didn't like that kind of thing. The pilot of the seaplane had room for four people, and he took two other passengers who we didn't know. The plane went out, circled around, and landed at a ramp at Boston Harbor. Oh, I loved flying, right from the beginning!

One of my favorite Alaska stories involves flying, and the Southeast Alaska area where we were on Crillon. At the time, our pilot Gene Meyring and Bob Ellis were the two best flyers in Alaska.

In those days, before Alaska had become a state, the president of the United States selected the governor of the Alaska Territory. Well, the governor had been selected, and apparently nobody liked him. Bob Ellis—who operated out of Ketchikan—was in Juneau with his wife, Peg, and their baby son, waiting for the arrival of a new engine. Peg had the baby lying on a crate, and was changing his diaper when the governor got off another plane and walked up to them and tickled the baby's tummy. The baby peed right in the governor's eye! Bob Ellis said, "My young son was the only man in Alaska who had the guts to do what everybody else in Alaska wanted to do!" Years later, however, that governor, Ernest Gruening, had become one of the most beloved state officials in Alaska's history.

Top: Pilot Gene Meyring and his Lockheed Vega seaplane at Crillon Lake base camp, August 1934. Flying with Gene helped us establish the climbable route to the summit. *Bottom:* The 1934 Harvard-Dartmouth Mount Crillon Expedition at base camp. Back row, from left: David Putnam, Russ Dow, Bob Stix, Bem Woods, Wok Holcombe. Middle row, from left, pilot Gene Meyring, Brad Washburn, Link Washburn (no relation), Hal Kellogg, Dick Goldthwait. In front, Ad Carter and Ted Streeter.

have been apparent. You knew the kind of people with whom you worked well and who enjoyed working together. Each time you planned a trip you had better people, better equipment, more experience.

Some people say I am the type of person who is always organized—but you should see my office! And—according to everyone else—I must be the type of person who always has to be in charge. Actually, I would have gladly gone on someone else's expedition if they had asked me. But I got the reputation of being a leader, and I think that other people began to feel that they wouldn't want me to be there trying to lead their expedition.

When we went to Fairweather in 1930, I realized we had bitten off more than we could chew. Certainly, in the early days of Alaskan exploration and climbing, lots of boldness was needed. Unlike many of the guys who went to Alaska, I had climbing experience in the Alps on snow and ice, and that was an asset. For Fairweather, I didn't really have a master plan for picking the other members of the group. I invited them because I knew them well and they were good outdoorsmen. Over time I began thinking more about the composition of a team and what each member brought to it in terms of skills and expertise in mountaineering. For example, Charlie Houston (who'd had a room near me in Lowell House, where I had spent my sophomore year at Harvard) was with us on Crillon in 1933. He was an expert climber—in 1934, he organized his own trip and made the first ascent of 17,400-foot Mount Foraker in the Alaska Range, a terrific feat. Charlie and my good friend Bob Bates organized the American trip to K-2 later in the 1930s. Having Bob Bates in a party was always a good thing.

On the third Crillon trip we flew in before the equipment arrived. Flying out to base camp from Juneau with Gene Meyring in a Lockheed Vega, I had the most wonderful plane ride of my life. Icy Strait was clear, with silvery seas of clouds to the west and north, and the whole Fairweather Range silhouetted against the pale evening sky. Hal Kellogg, an expedition member from New York, thought the mountains were a mirage.

We had eleven members in the group—with four from Harvard and four from Dartmouth—and it didn't seem quite real that I was back at Mount Crillon in the third week of June for an extended stay once again. But what a grand feeling it was to be back with the old glacier cracking, the wind singing in the trees, and the water lapping on the shore! The thrushes were simply glorious, singing so hard and steadily that they almost kept us from sleeping.

Once we were settled at base camp we tried the risky business of an air drop to 5,600 feet, a camp site we called The Knoll, with no one manning it. We loaded the Lockheed Vega with thirty-one boxes and bundles. The mechanic and I rode in the rear of the plane, with the door off. The plane was so full that I had to crouch with my knees against my chin, and hold a box from falling on top of me as we taxied down the lake to take off.

The first box went out and sailed gradually downward, turning over and over in the air for what seemed an interminable time. First it looked as if it would surely fall into a crevasse. Finally, after a ten-second plunge, it buried itself safely in the slushy snow and without breaking, exactly where we wanted it to fall.

One box got stuck in the door and didn't go out until an instant too late. It just barely missed hitting a pinnacle of rock, completely cleared the snowfield, and hurtled out of sight down a fifty-degree snow gully walled by crags of rock that dropped all the way to the valley below.

The next day we climbed up to retrieve the supplies. Boxes lay everywhere around us, each in a crater about eighteen inches

The key to the ascent of Crillon was the ascent of the 800-foot "Ice Cliff." Getting across this big crack at the bottom of the cliff, known as a "bergschrund," was the key to the key! Charlie Houston is here about to climb on top of Bob Bates, while Ad Carter waits below with several wooden "pickets" onto which fixed ropes were later to be attached, to make the descent of this awesome slope safer and simpler.

deep. Russ Dow and I headed for the big gully to try to retrieve the box that had dropped so dramatically into it. I peeked down the chute, and there it was just ten feet below me, but I didn't dare go for it without a rope. Almost everything else landed safely and was easy to find. Only six or seven cans had been ruined. We took a long rope and had no difficulty retrieving the lone box out of that gully.

Stuck at the Great Valley Camp (our third Crillon camp) on July 18, zowie, did we have a funny breakfast! I had eaten six bowls of oatmeal and was lying on my bed to recuperate and prepare myself for more labors, when Hal Kellogg asked for some water to wash out his cereal cup. I passed it over and spilled a bit on Waldo Holcombe's foot. Wok, as we called him, jumped and spilled about half his coffee on his pants, scalding his leg. Whereupon I jumped because I was surprised, and I spilled even more of Wok's coffee on him. He yelled with pain and leaped high in the air, hitting the tent and knocking down all the water that had condensed on the roof from cooking. Henry Woods from Dartmouth, nicknamed Bem, came in and we started laughing so hard explaining what happened that Wok kicked over the rest of his coffee!

It was July 19, shortly past midnight, when we began what turned into a thirteen-hour assault on the summit of Crillon.

We were out of camp at 2:00 A.M. The weather was so perfect, the night so clear and cold, and the crust so hard that when we reached the South Col at 3:10 A.M., we decided at once to have a wholehearted stab at the Ice Cliff that led us upward toward Crillon's summit. We stopped at our cache of four days before to pick up ice creepers, extra ropes, axes, and food. Then we skied to the base of the cliff on the most divine snow imaginable, a hard crust with about two-millionths of an inch of soft, fluffy, frost surface. The cliff looked more formidable than ever, studded with outcrops of rock that had not been exposed the year before. We roped up in three groups. Bem went with me, Ad Carter and Hal followed close behind, and Wok Holcombe and Ted Streeter waited until we found out what was ahead.

It was my job to lead. We were well-equipped with long ropes; if we succeeded in reaching the top we intended to fix permanent lines all of the way up the cliff, above which was a huge plateau beneath the summit. We would need them on the way down, because we were bound to be terribly fatigued from the ascent. Shortly before 7:00 A.M., while balancing on Bem's shoulders, I poked my head slowly through the excavations we had made. I jabbed my ice axe deep into the firm snow above us. We had reached the great plateau that led to the top of Mount Crillon.

We had come two thousand vertical feet in six hours, with forty-five hundred still to go, when the six of us held a council of war. This was as far as we had planned to go on that day, but the weather was so perfect we decided to try for the top. Ad Carter and I were the most experienced climbers; we roped together and took all of the chocolate and lemon drops, and I borrowed Bem's snow goggles. At the start, we found really easy hiking on that huge plateau.

In just over an hour and a quarter we were at the base of Crillon's summit cone. Over the last four thousand feet, Ad had led with a superb pace, steady, short steps, the kind that get one up fast. At ten seconds before 12:30 P.M., we planted our axes atop the peak of Mount Crillon and shook hands until our wrists ached. We both shouted with glee.

With the weather deteriorating, our stay on top was short. The snowy conditions also made it impossible for the others to follow us up that day. Back at camp, however, I made a

Just before reaching the final camp with a big load, we rested briefly, with Crillon towering 6,700 feet above us.

horrifying discovery: the lens on my camera was loose. I was sure all of my high-altitude pictures had been ruined. The only solution was to climb Crillon again, and soon, while our tracks were still clear.

The next day, Ad, Wok, and I made the climb the second time. At the summit it was cool, with a little breeze swirling bits of loose snow in our faces. We unrolled an American flag and a Harvard banner and lashed them to a ski pole. We took pictures until our fingers ached from changing film.

It was thrilling for us to see a view that no one had ever seen. The top was absolutely flat, about thirty-by-forty feet in diameter. We got as near to the edge as we dared. Ad stuck his ice axe and my ice axe together to give us real safety, then I crawled on my belly and looked down that five-thousand-foot cliff on Crillon's northwest face. It was a helluva view.

The only injury in all of my trips to Alaska—an amazing record, and a lucky one—happened on that 1934 trip to Crillon. Ted Streeter got badly hurt when we were coming down the peak from higher camps with big loads. We were near the end of the trip, and I said at the top of a steep slope, "I think we ought to go to the left. I think it's safer to descend that way." We had huge loads on our backs, maybe ninety pounds. Ted went the other way, then all of a sudden, he went head-over-heels right past me. It was a miracle that he didn't knock me over. He fell all the way to the bottom of the steep slope we were descending, and he lost a finger when he hit a rock that cut it right off.

I never said, "You damned fool"—which would have been very easy to do. What he did was indeed very foolish, trying to take a shortcut that didn't pay off. When you're the leader, you've got to hope that everybody else will go where you tell them. That was the only time on any of my trips that somebody made an awful mistake—and he paid for it with a lost finger.

After we got back I wrote a long story about our trips to Crillon for *National Geographic*, which appeared in the March 1935 issue, with forty-two pictures and maps.

By then, of course, I was hooked on Alaska, and wanted to keep going back.

Geologist Dick Goldthwait and his seismic-sounding apparatus on South Crillon Glacier. The ice depth here was 840 feet. This was the first time that seismic measurements had been taken on an Alaska glacier.

The first freight landing of the expedition's Fokker Super Universal ski-plane on Lowell Glacier, May 5, 1935.

CHAPTER SEVEN

THE NATIONAL GEOGRAPHIC YUKON EXPEDITION

After we climbed Mount Crillon, I thought about where to go next. I knew that the highest unclimbed mountain in North America was Mount Lucania in the same region, near the Alaska–Canada border. Bob Bates and I put together a team to climb the 17,150-foot mountain in 1935.

When word got around about what we were planning, I received a telephone call from Bill Ladd, one of the top guys in the American Alpine Club. I was just a kid and he was one of the hotshots, and he said, "You can't go to Lucania. Walter Wood is going to do it, and you'd better back out of your plan and let him try first."

Walter Wood was a very important mountaineer. He had a pile of money, so when he went on a trip he paid the bill himself. He didn't ask Harvard or the National Geographic for financial help. Walter could select who went with him and exactly how they would climb. He was a big name, so we backed off.

We had a team of seven—Adams Carter was among them— but instead of staying home, I said, "Let's go into the same area. It's enormous." There was a six-thousand-square-mile area that was empty on the map. Nearly thirty years before, the National Geographic had sent a group to map the area, but for three decades the job of completing the survey, in the St. Elias Mountain Range region near the Alaska–Canada border, lay unfinished. We weren't going to climb anything, but we were going to fill in as many of the blanks as possible, and the National Geographic agreed that this was a worthwhile thing to do. So we became the National Geographic Yukon Expedition.

This was a terrific expedition that involved a lot of hard work and logistical planning. It was an enormous undertaking just to get the supplies where we needed them. We placed a huge reliance on airplanes. Our experience using an airplane on Mount Crillon the year before proved to be a phenomenal help during the Yukon Expedition.

One of our great pilots was Bob Randall. The trip started in the winter and we landed on skis. (In those days, wheels were removed from Bush planes and skis were attached for snow landings. This was long before the combination ski wheels were used.) It helped that I was a pilot and could relate to the pilots who we hired. It wasn't that I had a lot of hours in the air, but I knew how to fly, knew what the airplanes could do, and understood pilots. For that reason, I don't think the pilots I flew with in the Alaska wilderness looked at me strangely when I made a suggestion, or thought that what I was proposing was too far out.

One time we were way up to the edge of nowhere and Bob Randall turned to me and said, "Where in hell are we?" The whole area was unmapped and we were flying over a sea of white, snow-covered land and glaciers. You had to have a good mental picture of where you were. I said, "Bob, don't worry. I know where we are. I know how to get out of this place." And we did.

Bastion Peak camp and dog team, National Geographic Yukon Expedition of 1935.

The Yukon Expedition began in February 1935 and didn't conclude until June. We took the train across the country from

---

These were exciting times to be flying. When you fly over that country nowadays in a jet airplane, people don't even bother looking out of the window. In those days, it was thrilling. You were never very high; the airplanes weren't powerful enough to get much higher than the tops of the mountains. It was a thrilling ballgame to be flying and mapping country that nobody had seen before.

Flying in the north often produced unusual experiences. Some years later my wife, Barbara, and I were flying from Alaska back to Boston. We were headed from Whitehorse in the Yukon to Winnipeg, but we had to switch planes in Edmonton. When we got to Edmonton there were no seats available on the next flight. Bob Randall lived in Edmonton and we called him up for lunch at the airport.

Then he got on the telephone and found us a free flight to Winnipeg, though he warned us that the pilot was taking the plane to Winnipeg because the radio was broken. Barbara and I got on the plane and, after an hour or so of flying, the copilot came back and asked if we wanted a soft drink. I said, "Sure." But he didn't come back with the drink. After about thirty minutes, the plane started descending, and we landed in Saskatoon. We taxied to the edge of the airport—right up to the area where we could buy a cold drink! Then we resumed the flight. Those were the wonderful early days of commercial aviation, when everybody knew and trusted everybody else.

Boston, through Chicago, North Dakota, Montana, and on to Seattle. Once in the Seattle area I drove to Mount Rainier, at 14,410 feet one of the tallest mountains in the Lower 48 states. At 4,800 feet the snow was piled on the road higher than car level. I walked more than a mile to the lodge at Paradise, which is larger than the Summit House on Mount Washington. At Paradise the snow level was 120 inches, and the drifts rose right over the 25-foot gable of the roof. And they were complaining about a lack of snow! They said it was usually more than 200 inches.

In late February, Andy Taylor and I took an exploratory flight with Everest Wasson in his Fairchild FC-2W2 out of Carcross, Yukon Territory. It was a glorious morning. The sun had just risen when we started down a runway that was marked by spruce boughs stuck in the snow on Lake Bennett. We could see Mount Crillon and Mount Fairweather far to the south, as we flew along at 12,000 feet. The shadows were deep and beautiful, and occasional soft mists hung in the valleys. Neither Andy nor I had ever seen such rough country in our lives—and we'd seen plenty of roughness.

Andy and I set up our first temporary camp on the lower part of what was later called the Lowell Glacier, named after the distinguished Harvard president Abbot Lawrence Lowell. The next day it was 14 degrees below zero, and storming on the mountains around us. I guess we had been lucky on our first reconnaissance flight.

It was a young team. I was not yet twenty-five, and except for Andy (who was sixty, and had been a member of the party that made the first ascent of Mount Logan), no one else was older. Bob and Ad and I had been together on quite a number of snowy climbs. Ome Daiber was an experienced mountaineer from Seattle, and Harty Beardsley was from Vermont. Jack

Haydon was our dog driver any time we could get him from Kluane at a charge of $5 a day.

After a steady diet of moose steaks and other variations of moose meat through the end of February at Carcross, we transferred all of the supplies and men to the Lowell Glacier on a big Fokker Super Universal plane. It was 45 below zero at our new camp. We had to scurry to get the plane unloaded before the engine froze and Wasson got stuck with us. A Logan tent went up in a jiffy, and then the big base-camp wall tent that looked as if we had used it at every camp for a year. After a frugal lunch of nuts, cake, and hot coffee from a heaven-sent Thermos bottle, two more Logan tents went up.

A series of recon flights followed with Bob Randall. I used a small Fairchild F-8 camera. Every time we crossed the mountains we saw interesting and beautiful things. The millions of old cirques and jagged, crenelated ridges and sharp peaks held new secrets no matter how many times we crossed them.

The Yukon Expedition was the first time I blended flying and mountain photography. I wasn't the first person to do this. In the late 1920s or early 1930s, the U.S. Forest Service, using seaplanes, traveled along the coast taking pictures. Once we began using airplanes on Mount Crillon, I could see the potential. This became a very important part of my work; and one that I enjoyed very much. I began taking the door off the side of the planes to shoot my photos and I tied a rope around my waist to hold myself in the plane. Later, I began using a chain that hooked to a carabiner snapped on the back of the airplane, and ran through my belt. Lots of people said, "How would you dare do it?" I wasn't worried.

I tied myself in partially so I wouldn't fall out and partially so I could lean forward and get straight-down pictures. Then people asked, "Well, how the hell did you get back in?" I told

Pilot Bob Randall and I with my small Fairchild F-8 camera, used to take all of the photographs made on the Yukon Expedition for National Geographic.

them it was very simple. If I was hanging out the door, all I had to do was pull that rope back up to get back in. There was never a close call. It had to work—I tied the knots. People react even more to it today than they did back then, because it's something nobody does now. Of course, only a couple of us were doing it in 1935.

A great deal relied on the pilot. I could tell him how to maneuver. I would say, "Give it a little bit more rudder." Or, "Give it a little bit more stick." That gave him confidence that I knew what I was talking about, and I wasn't telling him something stupid. The pilots didn't give a rip about photography. They were just doing it because the National Geographic Society paid them to do it, and they wanted to get back on the ground safely.

The third week in March we established our Cascade Camp. We had a 6 x 6 x 6 prefabricated beaverboard hut there, and we flew Jack Haydon and the dogs in from nearby Kluane Lake. It took until the last days of March to get the whole crew together there because of frequent weather delays. Zeus, it was grand to be there! There was great good humor and swell morale. After a grand supper—golly, codfish cakes are good, and so is currant jelly—Andy and I carefully cleaned our surveying instrument, a theodolite loaned to us by Harvard's Institute for Geographical Exploration. Theodolites are used to accurately measure vertical and horizontal angles, and ours was an excellent British Tavistock instrument.

After getting base camp established, we put in our baseline station. We worked steadily, but we were almost constantly interrupted by snowstorms. We were not far from the coast, and—unlike in the Alaska Interior—they were big, moist, warm blizzards that piled up deep snow very fast. We were often stuck inside, reading or playing cards all day. Once, we played for the stakes of a box of peanuts. That doesn't sound like much, but the loser had to go outside in the storm and get the nuts from our buried food cache. Ome lost, and thereafter he was the only man in camp who wouldn't touch peanuts.

At times we had remarkable radio reception. We heard a news report direct from Bordeaux, France, and we heard the New York radio show *Amos and Andy*. On the eve of Easter Sunday, April 21, we went to sleep with the wind blowing furiously, yet we were peacefully awakened by the singing of birds— I could not get over the contrasts of that land. The next day, with the arrival of a plane, I did some aerial surveying and photography. We swung around the southern side of Mount Hubbard, then turned northward over the mass of unknown peaks east and north of Mount Vancouver. We ran through the pass between Mount Walsh and Mount Lucania, getting simply glorious pictures.

We turned south again, up the valley of a great, unnamed glacier that came eastward from Mount Walsh. We passed one area of this glacier that heads up to the south of Walsh, and we continued to where it and the Kaskawulsh Glacier and the Hubbard Glacier merge in one great snowfield 8,000 or so feet high. A big snow mound—scarcely a mountain, really—at least 12,500 feet high, rises from this snowfield. We later named this peak Mount Queen Mary. We swung about to its left, taking a picture of a peak that rises to 12,000 feet or so in a stupendous pinnacle of rock and ice, and we named that one Mount King George. The peaks were named in honor of the British monarchs, marking the twenty-fifth anniversary—the silver jubilee—of King George V's ascension to the throne. They became known as the Jubilee Peaks.

One of the great advantages of having an airplane going back and forth to Carcross while we were in the field was the ability to send the photo negatives out to be developed. When the plane returned, we soon had pictures to use in our surveying. We worked whenever we could, between snowstorms. Only two days after this last photo flight, we were socked with another terrific southwester. You couldn't predict when you would get a storm, or have any idea how long it would last. Our little house shook and quivered with every blast of wind, and the snow came by horizontally.

Two days later, despite screaming wind, we decided to advance to Bastion Camp, also on the Lowell Glacier. The going was terrible, with deep, new powder snow, but we were determined to push through if it was humanly possible. We hauled two loads up the hill in the morning and one in the afternoon. It took another two days for us to reach our final camp at 8,300 feet, at the very foot of the 6,000-foot cliffs of East Hubbard (which is now known as Mount Kennedy).

Our dinner reward, after we set up four survey stations, was bear meat. The grand supper came from a bear shot by the boys on a foray down through Dusty Creek Valley. It certainly tasted good to eat something chewy, but most of the meat was eventually fed to the dogs. It seemed that every time we tried to move, or to survey, we faced 30 mph winds and drifting snow. When we packed up at high camp in early May, the dogs were a great asset. They pulled our load back down into Bastion Camp at a trot, as if it weighed nothing.

When we dropped down to Cascade Camp, Jack, Bob, and I traveled with a four-hundred-pound sledge load through snow that was deep, sticky, and fresh. The sled must have turned over a thousand times in the nine miles from Bastion Camp, and when we finally got home Jack claimed it was the worst trail he'd ever mushed over. All praise to the dogs—they were magnificent. Supper was fantastic: cold tomato juice, bear

Ad Carter and I surveying from a rock ledge aside the Lowell Glacier, a rocky little island in an ocean of ice and snow.

meat hamburgers, creamed corn, thick mushroom soup, and to cap it off, a juicy fig pudding. Being back at the hut made us think of how close we were to the ocean, and of moving on to Yakutat, our disembarkation point. Then we got socked by another terrific snowstorm and all feelings of spring fever were banished.

Another day passed and Jack and his dogs headed up to Bastion Camp to haul a final load of gear. Harty and I went along to finalize some surveying. The dogs, each hitched in his harness, frolicked gaily all about us. It was marvelous how much excess energy those dogs always seemed to have. We had just reached the crest of the first steep pitch one hundred feet above camp, when the pups went tearing off to our right, leaping and playing, chasing a dog named Cracker. Normally we kept the dogs tied to an empty sled, but this time we had let them loose— clearly a mistake. All of a sudden I saw one tail in the air, disappearing down through a narrow slit in the snow, and then there were only three dogs in sight! Jack rushed toward the spot, at the very edge of a great crack only a hundred feet or so to our right. I yelled to him to watch out.

We grabbed the three remaining dogs, who were whining and running about aimlessly above a tiny hole. Tex, Cracker, and Tip were okay. Brownie, Fannie, and Monkey were nowhere to be seen. We ran over as near the hole as we dared. Then, well-roped, we crawled on our hands and knees and peered into it. We were already nearly to our waists over a vast crack with a completely snowed-over top. Jack called wildly, "Brownie! Brownie!" Not a sound came from below us. The crack went straight down for thirty feet, and then, amid a mass of jagged slices of ice, it twisted toward us and went out of sight under us into the deep blue-green of the bowels of the glacier. We called again. "Fannie! Brownie! Monkey!" Not a sound. I was afraid that all three of them were dead. God, what a crack. I'd never seen such a formidable crevasse, with all its jagged walls.

Bob Bates was lashing his load down below, and we yelled to him to bring up a rope. He picked up a coil and rushed up the forty-five-degree pitch. Harty left his load a hundred yards ahead of us, and sped back down to help. When Bob got there, we staked in a pair of skis at a safe distance from the edge of the hole and made the rope fast. Listen and call as we did, not a murmur came from below. I tied myself on one end of the rope, and we tied the other end to the skis—it was a hundred-foot rope. We let the loop of slack down into the hole and I hitched up in rappel and slid over the edge of the snow, through the narrow hole that the pups had made, into the upper vault of the chasm. For the first twenty feet, the walls were hard-packed winter snow. Chunks of the lip of the crack kept falling on my head as I descended. The ice walls of the crack were covered with dog crap. Those poor dogs were literally scared shitless.

At twenty or so feet down, it was clear that the dogs must have glanced off to my right, and far down a deep grotto that ran below me, out of sight. Given where the rope was hitched above, it would not have been safe to try to descend further, for it would probably have dislodged some of the huge, loose slabs of ice that had apparently crashed from the lip of the crack a week or so ago and jammed very precariously just below me.

I wedged myself crosswise between the icy walls and yelled for the men to move the skis and rope ten or twelve feet over to my right, and then call down to me. There was scuffling up above, and lots of snow fell down my neck. Otherwise, I couldn't hear a sound. I've never known a more hopeless feeling than to be jammed thirty feet below the surface in a cold, clammy crack with a loose, useless rope dangling above me. Then a reassuring

Ad Carter and the dogs negotiating a very steep pitch of the Lowell Glacier Icefall, just above our base camp.

yell came. A new hole had to be smashed above me through which to pass the rope, and that caused more loose snow to fall on me. The rope tightened and I started down again. Deeper and deeper I descended. The light got dimmer as I started sliding off, down under the overhang.

Far below me in the grayness I saw something move. Splotches of blood stained the ice walls beside me. I called, "Monkey!" There was no reply, but there was a faint movement in response. As my eyes grew more accustomed to the scant light, I could see all three of the dogs, lying on top of one another. Fannie was on the bottom, Brownie in the middle, and Monkey on top. They were huddled in a shivering mass on a little heap of shattered ice that filled the very bottom of the crevasse. They were still thirty feet below, and I didn't dare move another inch until I pulled off a huge, loose chunk of ice that was clinging, by God knows what, to the wall just below me—and that would surely be knocked off onto either the dogs or me if I couldn't remove it.

I called up for the others to hold even tighter, and bracing myself securely, I pulled off the chunk and tossed it down a deep chasm beyond the dogs. It clattered from wall to wall for a second, and then crashed with a resounding roar far below in the dark depths. The rope wasn't nearly long enough to reach the dogs, and I didn't want to have them pulled out above me for fear that they might knock ice down on my head as they were hauled up.

Bob Bates arrived with a hundred more feet of rope, after I'd waited what seemed an age. The dogs were still moving. The cracked ice and snow that covered them and lay around them in their narrow dungeon was splattered with blood. I pictured reaching them and finding them terribly injured. What a horrible job if I had to pull one out with a broken back, or even worse, had to kill him in front of his brothers rather than let him suffer.

The new rope arrived and I speedily made the last descent. It was no place to linger, with tons of loose blocks of ice hanging just above me, all ready to fall to the bottom of the crack at the slightest movement of the glacier. I quickly slipped a noose of the new rope through the harness of each dog, then I called, "Okay!" And I started up, nine-tenths being hauled and one-tenth hauling myself on the fixed rope. Monkey gave me one last pitiful glance and I was out of sight into the upper grotto, and then crawling out over the lip of the crack into the beautiful warm sunlight of our early May morning.

Andy arrived with his movie camera as we started to haul the dogs out. Just after we started there was a little jerk and the load lightened a lot—one of the harnesses must have broken. Which one was it? How far had he fallen? In a jiffy, the little forms of two dogs came over the edge of the crevasse, and we dragged Fannie and Brownie out onto the snow to safety. They were terrified to the point of utter silence, and they shivered with cold. Jack felt them all over as the other three dogs, tethered to a ski pole, watched quietly and intently. Nothing seemed to be radically wrong with the two hauled out, but what about poor Monkey, who now had fallen twice down that hole?

I had had all I wanted of the crevasse, so Ad Carter went down after Monkey, and I rushed down to the camp for another movie camera. I got back just in time to get a marvelous picture of Ad coming out, and Monkey, bedraggled but still alive, reaching the surface. What a magnificent bit of luck! I will never understand how those pups could fall at least seventy feet through that maze of jagged and torn ice and come out with nothing more than two cut lips (Brownie and Fannie) and one lost toenail (Monkey).

That was the great drama of the trip, but we weren't home free. On the retreat toward Yakutat, we were pounded repeatedly by storms. On May 23 I wrote in my expedition diary that it had snowed for seventy-three straight hours. Almost seventy years later, I can say that in my life I never saw bigger storms, with greater snowfall, than I did on the Yukon Expedition of 1935.

As we made our way off the ice for the first time in eighty days, we had to thread our way through a constant barrage of little snow avalanches and rocks as big as fists falling from cliffs. As Andy Taylor and I neared the waters of Nunatak Fjord, the bombardment grew worse. The sun rose higher in the sky, melting more snow and loosening more debris on us. That night I asked Andy if he had been scared. He replied in such a vivid manner that I understood he had been more frightened than the dogs were in the crevasse.

Andy and I paddled our inflatable boat triumphantly into Yakutat on May 30. A day later, at the radio shack, I received many congratulations from our families and friends. Suddenly, the radio operator shoved back his chair and cried out, "Jesus Christ, this message is from the King!"

The message was signed by the British foreign secretary, and read, "The King commands me to express to you the sincere appreciation of the compliment which the National Geographic Society Yukon Expedition have paid to his Majesty and the Queen in naming two newly discovered peaks after their majesties in commemoration of his silver jubilee. The King congratulates the expedition on their important achievement effecting the first crossing of the Saint Elias Range from Yukon to Alaska."

To save money, I spent some of the last nights in Yakutat sleeping on Bob Randall's floor. On June 6, I received a telegram from Dr. Gilbert Grosvenor, president of the National

Geographic Society. It read, "Heartiest congratulations to you and every member of your courageous and resourceful group. Your successful accomplishment of extremely difficult explorations as originally planned reflect greatest credit on every individual in your party."

My twenty-fifth birthday, June 7, was celebrated in the Yukon, together again with the entire team, which had taken various routes and methods to reach Whitehorse. The Yukon Expedition had discovered a new, fifty-mile long glacier, descending from Mount Hubbard to the Alsek Valley in the Yukon; found two new mountains—the Jubilee Peaks; and learned that the Hubbard Glacier was at least twice as long as the thirty miles previously thought. (I also took terrific pictures of Mount Lucania, which would prove to be very useful.)

A few months after completion of the Yukon Expedition, I was invited to give a speech to the members of the Canadian Geographical Society in Ottawa. To my amazement and delight, I was invited to be the guest of Lord Tweedsmuir, John Buchan, then Governor General of Canada. Those were the days when lecturers at an event like this wore a white tie and tails. I borrowed a tie, trousers, and tails from a friend, and thrilled, headed for Ottawa on the night train from Boston.

I was met, officially, at the station by the Governor General's automobile, and, after a late tea with his lordship and several guests, I headed for my room to dress for a State Dinner and my Yukon Expedition lecture. A uniformed butler had hung my clothes in a closet. I encountered no major difficulty in putting on the starched front shirt and new, white tie. But then, to my horror, I discovered that I could not use a belt to hold up my trousers. I had to have suspenders!

Only fifteen minutes remained before I had to go to dinner and I was frantic—until I spied a broad fabric belt that hung

The discovery of Mount Kennedy, 8:00 A.M., May 1, 1935, then known as East Hubbard. This magnificent peak wasn't officially named Kennedy until 1963, at the time of the president's death.

on the wall near the door. I pulled it hard and waited for a response. In no time at all, a liveried butler arrived and warned me that it was only ten minutes to dinner. He was also horrified when I described my predicament.

"I've got to get some suspenders and get them in a big hurry," I said. "I can't loan you mine," he said, "because I've got to serve at the dinner. But I'll dash down and get you the cook's." He left on the run, but returned almost immediately with the bad news that the cook was ill and had gone home, suspenders and all.

"However," the butler said, "somehow, I'll get some braces for you and leave them here on your bed between courses of your dinner. Somehow, sir, you'll have to find an excuse to get back up here for a moment after dinner, before you have to go downtown with His Excellency for your speech. God alone knows how you'll manage during dinner, which starts in a very few moments."

The trousers I had borrowed were rather tight at the waist, so I decided to risk it and hurried downstairs with neither a belt nor suspenders. In order to avoid having my pants fall off, however, I had to keep one hand in a pants pocket throughout the drinks with several distinguished guests. It was worrisome, but it worked, though it was very bad manners to keep a hand in a pocket when meeting exquisitely mannered guests before a state dinner.

Once seated at Lord Tweedsmuir's right, I heaved a massive sigh of relief and made it through dinner. Then, using the excuse that I had left the slides for the lecture upstairs, I dashed up, and there on my bed was the best set of suspenders I had ever seen.

The next morning at breakfast I told the tale of the missing braces to Lord Tweedsmuir, and he roared with laughter.

Chapter Eight

Meeting Mount McKinley and Amelia Earhart

The following year, in the June issue, the *National Geographic* published my account of the Yukon Expedition, with many photographs—they were very happy with how it turned out. I also lectured on the Yukon Expedition at the Royal Geographic Society in London.

After we had made a big success out of the expedition, I got a call from Gilbert Grosvenor and he asked, "Brad, is there anything else out there that you could do that wouldn't cost too much money and hasn't been done?"

I thought for a minute and told him that I had just the thing: "Nobody has ever taken aerial photographs of Mount McKinley in Alaska." He said, "I'll give you $1,000." So we made the first flights in a Lockheed Electra in September 1936, and produced the first large-format, 8 x 10 photographs of McKinley. That was the first time I saw Mount McKinley and boy, it made an impression on me—the way it stood out above the other mountains around it. Not only did we make the flights and the pictures, but I gave Dr. Grosvenor a refund of $40. It wasn't much, but I came in under budget.

As it turned out, the use of that particular airplane led to another unusual incident. One day I got a phone call from

No one had made aerial photographs of Alaska's Mount McKinley until September 1936, when we made the first flights in a Lockheed Electra. Here, a huge thunderstorm dies out on the mountain's southern face. Ansel Adams claimed this McKinley image was his favorite Washburn photograph.

George Putnam, my old publisher, and he asked me to come to his house in Rye, New York. He was married to the famous pilot Amelia Earhart, who was planning to fly around the world. He called to ask me to spend the weekend with them, but said only that they had "something very interesting to discuss" with me.

I had never met Amelia, and found her just as charming and pleasant as I had heard she was. And she looked exactly as she had in all the pictures I had seen: tousled hair, boyish smile, pullover sweater, relaxed, informal, delightful. At supper, Amelia told me that she was putting together plans for a round-the-world flight in the summer of 1937, and that she was interviewing a number of people as possible navigators. They talked a lot about her plans, and threw out some ideas about the trip. I thought the idea was stupid to begin with, not the idea of flying around the world, but the idea of doing it in a Lockheed Electra without a copilot.

After supper we spread out a mass of maps on the living room floor, and Amelia and I sat on the floor while she described her plan in great detail. I saw a key flaw in her plan for navigation between Darwin, Australia, and Howland Island. (Howland Island is a sliver of land in an immense mass of trackless ocean, about a mile and a half long and a half mile wide.) I asked her how she planned to hit it at the end of a two-thousand-mile flight without a single, intermediate emergency landing spot. She replied: dead reckoning, and star and sun sights. We never even got to discussing where she was going to land: on a beach, or a small, specially prepared field. At that point I thought the problem wasn't landing, it was how to get there.

They made it seem as if they might be sounding out my interest to be the navigator, and people later said, "You turned her down." I said, "Nothing of the sort." She may have had that in mind, but it certainly was not expressed to me in that way.

I thought the whole thing was a bad idea because no one ever flew a twin-engine Electra without a copilot. It was crazy to take an airplane that had two seats up front, one for the pilot and one for the copilot, with nobody in the copilot's seat. Forget the navigator. If she got sick on one of the legs, the copilot could hold the controls. Anybody can fly an airplane for a while by turning the wheel or using the rudder while the pilot vomits. Then, when they recover sufficiently, they take over again and bring it in for a landing. So I thought it was a crazy idea.

I didn't get into suggesting another type of airplane. The big discussion that I got involved in was locating Howland Island. I said, "The one part of this flight that I'm very scared about, if I were to be involved, would be how you are going to find Howland Island." From Darwin, Australia, it was a thousand-mile leg. I knew that that airplane flew most economically to conserve fuel at an altitude of 12,000 feet. Suppose you got out there after a thousand miles. You knew the chances were very high that you'd have fractocumulus clouds—a mass of small, ragged clouds torn loose from cumulus clouds—each throwing a shadow on the surface of the water. Well, as you neared where you thought Howland Island ought to be, based on the passage of time, some of those clouds might begin to look like Howland Island.

What you needed was a radio on Howland Island. If you had somebody there who could talk to you on the radio, and let you know your position, that would be a big help. Or if you just had something that sent a signal, *dah-di-dah, dah-di-dah*, all day long, you could home in on that point. Without that, you needed to see the island to locate it. If you went down under the fractocumulus clouds and there wasn't an island, it was just a shadow, that would force you to fly back up to 12,000 feet, wasting a lot more fuel. I told her, "You've got to have a radio on Howland Island." Amelia insisted that it wasn't necessary.

I said that a big, complex radio installation wasn't at all necessary, just an automatic signal sent out continually. Any sort of signal that you could pick up with a Radio Direction Finder. If she had asked for a young radioman to do this she would have had hundreds of volunteers in a moment. In fact, she was so popular that I'm sure she would have found a score of very competent operators who would have paid her for the fun and privilege of doing it.

And that's where our discussion ended. When I finished, George made a comment I will never forget: "If you're going to all that trouble to get a radio there, the book will not be out for Christmas sales." He was essentially using Amelia's flight as a promotion for the book he was going to publish.

Amelia had no response to what I'd said. She didn't say, "I don't agree," or "I don't like that." Nothing. I went back home to Boston and never heard from George Putnam or Amelia Earhart again. As navigator, she chose Fred Noonan, a fellow who had navigated for Pan American's Pacific flights.

In 1937, flying from Burwash Landing to Fairbanks with the famous pilot Joe Crosson, I heard the news that Amelia Earhart had disappeared. As far as we know, Amelia and her navigator never made it to Howland Island. Why she refused to bring a copilot, why her radio planning and execution were so unsatisfactory, nobody will ever know. If I'd been asked, I'd have refused to go under the conditions planned. And a navigator who was far more experienced than I failed to do the job with the equipment at hand. Amelia Earhart's

I began doing graduate work at the Harvard Institute of Geographical Exploration in 1933, in the fall after I completed my undergraduate degree, and I stayed there until 1936, but I never really finished my graduate work at Harvard. However, I was awarded an M.A. in geology and geography from Harvard in 1960.

That year I was elected to the Board of Overseers of Harvard University. At one of our lunch breaks at the Harvard Faculty Club, I was talking with the secretary of the board. He asked, "Why didn't you ever get a graduate degree at Harvard?" I said, "It's very simple. To get a graduate degree at Harvard you had to know geologic German as well as French. I have a very good knowledge of geologic French, but not German. I can't speak a word of German."

A couple of months went by, and at another meeting the same fellow said, "I've been told that the requirements have changed and that if you speak geologic French, that's okay." I thought that was fine, and asked how I would go about actually obtaining the degree. He sent me to the head of the Department of Geology, Professor Cornelius Hurlbut. He said it was true that the requirements had changed, and all I had to do was prove that I understood geologic French. He wanted me to read a page or two to him. Since I hadn't studied or prepared, I asked what would happen if I failed. He said I would be able to try again. So I said, "I'll try it right now." I read him half a page of geologic French, and got my degree.

I never studied for a Ph.D. or earned a doctorate. I am

called Dr. Bradford Washburn from honorary titles. I received my first honorary doctorate from the University of Alaska in 1951, and by the time I was awarded my master's degree I had been given three more honorary doctorates: two from Tufts University and Colby College in 1957, and another from Northeastern University in 1958.

I had been told for years that you can't get an honorary Ph.D. from the University of Alaska. I've got more than a half-dozen others, so you can count any one you want if you consider the Alaska one illegal.

---

greatest liability was probably her extraordinary optimism, which in this situation exceeded the bounds of reason.

By 1936, I was returning to Alaska every year. The first time I saw Mount McKinley was when we flew over that September. My first impression was simple: big and beautiful. McKinley is different from Everest because it is all by itself. Everest is part of a big range with other huge peaks scattered right around it; McKinley is in a part of the Alaska Range where it, Mount Foraker, and Mount Hunter are the only three chunks of real estate that are separate and big.

This may come as a surprise, even though I was impressed by and admired McKinley's beauty right away, I did not immediately think I was going to climb it. I actually had zero thought that it was going to happen, until the U.S. Army sent me there to test winter equipment in the summer of 1942. I was busy doing other things.

At the end of the 1935 Yukon Expedition, I had Bob Randall fly out of his way so I could get pictures of Mount Lucania, just in case Walter Wood failed to get to the top. I knew he was going to try to reach the summit from Canada, and the way I wanted to do it was from Alaska, from the other side. I got some gorgeous pictures, and kept them in my hip pocket until I saw what happened with Walter Wood.

Walter Wood's party made the first ascent of nearby 16,664-foot Mount Steele, but he didn't get up Lucania. In 1937, I was well prepared to climb Mount Lucania.

We took the door off Bob Reeve's Fairchild 71 airplane in Valdez, Alaska, so it wouldn't hinder my aerial photography. Customized rigging bore the weight of my fifty-three-pound Fairchild K-6 camera.

CHAPTER NINE

THE GREAT LUCANIA ENTERPRISE

Climbing Mount Lucania with Bob Bates was the greatest adventure of my life.

It became an adventure, not just an expedition, when things went wrong and failed to conform to our plan. If we had simply climbed Lucania, there would have been no fuss, but we got stuck there, and had a helluva time getting out. Lucania is 17,150 feet tall, and we planned to climb it from the Alaska side with a four-man team after being flown in with our supplies by the legendary Alaskan pilot Bob Reeve. But things went wrong quickly.

The expedition began on May 30, 1937, when I boarded the train from Boston to Chicago, leaving ahead of the rest of the group. The team consisted of myself, Bob Bates, Russell Dow (who had been with me before in Alaska), and Norman Bright of Sunnyvale, California (a very strong two-mile runner). I reached Seattle in four days, after hopping an airplane flight in Missoula, Montana. I had a rendezvous in Seattle with my old friend and climbing partner Ome Daiber, and together we made a flight over Mount Rainier.

I spent my twenty-seventh birthday in Ketchikan, after a boat ride through the beginnings of the Inside Passage of the Gulf of Alaska. We had a cloudless day, from sunrise to sunset, not very common in rainy Ketchikan. We continued, and docked at Wrangell at eight o'clock in the evening, where I bought some ivory dogs and totem poles for my parents. The black silhouettes of the trees against the deep red of the northern sky were wonderful. I slowly began to realize that I was actually back in Alaska for the seventh time.

The boat continued on to Juneau. Once there I took a flight to explore the area of Southeast Alaska with which I was quickly becoming very familiar. We took photographs over Glacier Bay, Mount Fairweather, and Mount Crillon to test Eastman's new noncurling film. I also took pictures of the eastern approaches of unclimbed Mount Bertha, because I thought I might like to climb it some day. Mounts Hubbard, Lucania, St. Elias, and Vancouver all stood out tremendously in the distance.

Bob Bates and I reached Cordova on June 11 and met up with Bob Reeve and his wife, Tillie. Then we went on to Valdez, the jumping-off point for our expedition. Days were spent packing and readying the supplies for Bob Reeve to fly in to the base of Mount Lucania. He was going to ferry the climbers and gear on a couple of shifts.

Bob Bates and I took off with Bob Reeve at 1:15 P.M. for the first flight from "Mudville" (as I called Valdez) to the Walsh Glacier. We barely made it. We waded out to the plane through pools of water and mud. The plane's skis just cleared the ditch and tall eel grass at the end of the runway. The plane wobbled a bit. We banked gently out across the bay and climbed toward Thompson Pass. Bob turned around and grinned his wonderful grin from underneath his trademark rain hat.

It was a rough flight into a headwind, and even though we took pictures and admired the scenery—Mounts Sanford, Wrangell, and Blackburn loomed to our left, white and glittering and shadowless under the boiling noonday sun—we gave a lot of thought to the very jagged range before the Chitina River Valley. There were mighty few places there where one could land, even in a crisis.

We flew through cumulus clouds that hung in pennants, and into the wind. Our time was slow and we stayed low, at 6,000 feet. As we reached the end of the Chitina River, Reeve, who had been smoking about one cigarette a minute for the past hour, said, "We're licked, Brad. That stuff ahead is too low. We can't make her. We can go only about ten more minutes before I'll have too little gas to get home." I urged him to try. He eased off on the throttle as we started across the most godforsaken waste of ice and rocks I'd ever seen, the snout of the Chitina Glacier.

Up until then we could have landed almost anywhere by tossing out our extra gas cases as we descended and wrecking the plane. We probably would have walked away unhurt. But for the next twenty-five miles we could not have landed at all. I shall never forget that nauseating desolation of dying masses of ice, much of it half buried in growths of scrub alders, all of it veneered with a deep layer of reddish boulders and gravel. The valley walls on both sides were very steep rock and scree, snowless and bleak. Potholes full of horrid, muddy water filled every depression in the hellish sea of stagnant ice at the end of the Chitina and Logan Glaciers.

We had been flying for a little less than two and a half hours, and could see the clouds ahead in a black, unbroken ceiling, and we had about a 25 mph headwind. But then we saw the north wall of Lucania at last. Bates yelled, "There she is!" And there was a tiny, black dot on a smooth patch of snow amid wide fields of crevasses—the supply cache left there by Bob and Russ Dow in May.

The motor idled, the rigging hummed, and we lost altitude like lightning. Before we knew it, there was a soft swish, not even a jolt. Then came a sharp bump and we whisked past a tiny crevasse. We crossed two more black slits in the snow. The trip had taken us just under three hours. Reeve explained that we had had to land across the narrow crevasses since they were the only things that showed him the surface of the snow beneath the leaden sky. When I jumped out of that plane, I sank to my waist in a sea of Walsh Glacier slush.

We had only one pair of snowshoes on the plane. It would be suicidal to walk around the crevasse area without snowshoes, so I hustled off to the cache, three-quarters of a mile away, to get two more pairs. At once the two Bobs began gassing up the plane. The temperature was 40 degrees. We were surprised by the warmth and the unexpected deep slush. I tried to hurry, but was huffing and puffing since we had quickly gone from sea level to about 8,500 feet. The cache was surrounded by snow-covered cracks. Very gingerly and scared stiff, I approached it by a series of wide zigzags.

I was heading back down the trail when I heard the plane's motor start. I watched the plane advance toward me up the gentle grade, wallowing and roaring in the slush. Then, abruptly, the left wing slumped toward the snow, stopping only a yard from the ground. The motor roared louder and the wing sank to within a foot of the surface. The motor stopped. Reeve was mired in that damned slush.

We shoveled around the plane for forty minutes. Then we tied a rope to the tail and, pulling and jerking as Reeve revved the motor, we moved it out of the deep slush. Bob taxied the plane a couple of thousand feet higher on the glacier and stopped. There was no chance for him to take off that night and get back to Valdez. We spent another hour making ice blocks and putting them under the skis. Shockingly, it was starting to rain— it was that warm. Rain at over 8,000 feet in Alaska!

Then we made camp. Reeve and I each fell into small crevasses within ten feet of the tent; he was badly frightened by that experience. The whole place was riddled with crevasses. The next morning we ate cream of wheat and drank coffee, and loafed in the warmth of the sun until noon. There were oceans of slush. It was obvious that the plane was stuck until we got a freeze. And then we had a thunderstorm! We were as perplexed as any mortals could be; it was like having a snowstorm in the Sahara Desert.

We started to realize that even if Reeve got a surface hard enough for taking off, he would not be able to return with our climbing partners and land again, because of the slush. And he would not be able to come back and land later to pick us up. Bates and I might be in for a long walk. We thought it must be eighty miles over unmapped country to Burwash Landing at Kluane Lake in the Yukon—the only safe way of retreat. The whole expedition suddenly took on a survival aspect.

On the morning of June 21, after a new crust formed, Reeve tried to take off. The plane bumped and jounced along, right to the edge of a big mass of cracks at the extreme limit of the runway, and stopped. Bates and I rushed down to where the airplane was stuck at least a foot deep in slush. We tied a rope around the tail, turned the plane around, and headed it back up toward camp. We had not gone a hundred yards before the plane was halfway up to the wing tips in a big crevasse, buried in deep slush.

We dug for thirty minutes, got the plane moving, only to see it fall into a tremendous hole after three hundred yards of taxiing uphill. Even the propeller had burrowed in eighteen inches or so. We had to dig it out again, and this time it was a terror of a job. We dug and pulled for three hours.

We thought it absurd to try to take off again until we had rock-hard crust, even if it meant waiting a month. It was definitely dangerous to fool around on the thin crust that formed at 30 degrees. We needed it to be 25 degrees, if not 20. We would be only too happy for Reeve to get safely off to Valdez. It was a terrible shame for Russ and Norm not to be able to join us, but it was obvious that Bates and I would have to walk out into Canada. It was ridiculous for our partners and Reeve to risk their lives on another flight. Since the plane did not have a radio, we were already worried about what folks might be thinking.

It dropped into the twenties that night, and on the morning of June 22, Reeve finally lifted his plane off the thick crust. I had never seen a closer takeoff, and I never wanted to see another like it. Bob Bates and I yelled and yelled, just shrieked for joy. However, we were also left on the Walsh Glacier to get ourselves home. Lord knows we had enough food at our huge base-camp cache.

It was a curious feeling to be all alone, except for one other fellow, on a thoroughly rotten glacier, with eighty miles of mountains and an 11,000-foot divide between you and civilization. Bob said, "We'll know what it's like to be married after this trip." I was glad the other fellow was Bob because we were both more experienced than the other two guys—they hadn't spent time in glaciated wilderness as we had during the Yukon Expedition.

We made a reconnaissance and determined that the best way to go was up the Walsh Glacier to the pass connecting Lucania (to the west) and Mount Steele (to the east). We had enough food to feed four men for weeks, but we couldn't carry all of it with us, even with sixty-pound packs. We sifted through the gear and discarded many things, including my movie camera and my costly Fairchild F-8 aerial camera. We had too much gasoline and too much of everything; we simply couldn't carry enough with us.

Our plan was to haul fifty days of food to the bottom of the Steele ridge (the Basin Camp, as we called it), and then haul twenty-five days of rations to the Ridge Camp. If we needed more there, we could descend and get it. We made plans on how to trim the volume of our gear, slept long hours, and ate until we were stuffed. I felt bad when we threw away Russ's and Norm's carefully packed clothes. It either rained or snowed every day for a week, but on June 25 we sledged 325 pounds of equipment up the glacier.

We got lucky when the temperature dropped, creating a fresh crust, and we were able to transfer all of our supplies in two days. After that, our motto became, "Chuck it and we won't have to lug it!" We cut our rations repeatedly. We had eaten no meat at all except for a huge, four-pound Hormel ham that was delicious beyond words. We broke out a second ham, ate raisins, pea soup, applesauce, tea, cocoa, jam, and pilot crackers, and gorged on lemonade from our canteens. Ten days after landing we still had not been through one complete day without rain or snow. We had to plan carefully to avoid avalanches.

When the sky cleared, we obtained stupendous views of Lucania and the huge peaks on all sides of us. We made a new camp on July 1, and I thought we were in the most superb basin in Alaska. The six-thousand-foot walls of Lucania and Steele towered to the west and the east and the great serac wall of our ridge rose four thousand feet above us, almost vertically, it seemed, as great ice blocks silhouetted against the sky. The sun was powerful and we registered a temperature of 80 degrees! In the afternoon of July 2, the thermometer shot up to 114 degrees while it lay on the snow and we had to cover it to keep it from bursting. We were even worried about sunstroke. A couple of feet off the floor of the tent, the air felt like a furnace. Then, after the hottest afternoon in northern history, we had a good freeze. That helped us make the last two thousand feet, hauling supplies to ridge camp at 12,200 feet on July 3. We had taken to calling the saddle between Lucania and Steele "Shangri-la," and we were only a day's run from it.

We had intense heat again and got sunburned as lobsters, and then had snow again. One-third of our two-pound tin of butter became rancid from roasting in the sun inside a duffle bag. On July 4 we moved up to 13,500 feet, though Bob and I fell to our waists into half a dozen snow-covered crevasses. We were roped at all times and were not harmed. By late evening, the temperature was down to 10 degrees. Zeus, it was cold up there. We reached a new camp at 13,800 feet the next day—where it dropped to 2 degrees below zero. One more day's hauling and we made it to the plateau and set up a camp at about 14,000 feet on the big, level pass between Mount Lucania and Mount Steele.

Steele was about three miles to the east over easy slopes. We were probably a four-hour walk to Walter Wood's ridge, which meant that in case of emergency we had a fairly safe exit into Canada. The base of Lucania's nearest peak was about two and a half miles of what would be easy going—except for damnable powder snow. After all of our hard work, we were determined to climb Lucania. Snow conditions and weather were the only things that could now prevent that climb.

We planned to head toward Lucania at the first possible chance, but we figured on ten days at Shangri-la. We had twenty-five to thirty days of food left. We were low on sugar, butter, and cereal, but had plenty of dried beef, gravy, soup, beans, pilot crackers, and bacon. We also had dates, raisins, sardines, and cheese. There was a possibility we could replenish our supply at a cache left by Walter Wood at the base of Mount Steele on our way out.

We had certainly fought to get there, but the tension was relaxed. We knew that only a two-thousand-foot spur separated us from the downhill route to Burwash Landing, and there were no crevasses in our way.

On July 7 we left two packs loaded with eight days' worth of food, plus crampons and rope, in a duffle bag on a hill at the base of Lucania, and started our final four-thousand-foot climb. The trailbreaking for three and a quarter miles was very bad on our way over. That night the temperature dropped to minus 1. The sky cleared the next day, even if it was 0 degrees in the tent.

There wasn't a cloud anywhere near Lucania on the morning of July 9. Bob and I tackled the slope and recognized that we would never get anywhere if we could not make most of it on snowshoes; the snow was waist-deep flour. It was a battle: Bob took fifty steps, then I took fifty steps. We changed the lead every few minutes, with no rests at all.

After four hours, we hit the last slope below the col, which was a forty-degree sideslope of fathomless powder, veneered with an inch of rock-hard wind-crust. I tried walking on it, but went through to my waist, dropping my snowshoes, which by the grace of God lodged on a little lump of ice about ten feet down the slope. The only thing to do was to dig a trench eighteen inches wide for about a hundred yards, cutting away the crust so we could get a purchase for our snowshoes in the soft snow. I worked on the trench for an hour, then Bob led. After five and a half hours of work, we took a break to eat chocolate, dates, and raisins.

Then the snow became solid and wind-packed. We put on crampons and left the snowshoes with most of the food and one rucksack. The ridge leading up Lucania was steep. We had stunning views of Mount Logan to the left, and of Mount

The view of Lucania from inside our tent.

Bona, Mount Wood, and all of the northern peaks on our right. Finally, we stood on the last, lofty pass before reaching the top. About a mile away the summit beckoned across a gentle divide of snow, with one last steep pitch.

Because of the altitude we had to travel slowly. But as long as we took it gently we never noticed it at all. It seemed like a dream, Bob Bates and I approaching the very top of Lucania with no more difficulties in sight. At 4:30 P.M. we came over the top of what we had thought all along was the summit, ready to let out a yell of joy. We stepped out onto the frost-feathered cornice only to see another snowy mound just ahead of us. Ten minutes later our yell of triumph could have been heard in Timbuktu.

The top of Mount Lucania is a sharp ridge about thirty feet long. A scattering of fleecy clouds was all that blocked our view. Oh, that feeling of joy, of accomplishment, enriched by all the work we had put into reaching our goal!

After resting at Shangri-la for two days, we put in a cache at 15,000 feet, near the summit of Steele. Bob and I reloaded seventy-five-pound packs and then the serious work began. We spent an hour and a half working our way above 16,000 feet by inching to the shoulder of Steele. We snowshoed halfway up the final pyramid, put on our crampons, and reached the summit in almost a stroll. On July 11, we completed the second ascent of Mount Steele.

The top of Steele is very beautiful; formed of a cluster of three little frost-feather–covered humps. The highest one has a nice, flat top about fifteen by twenty feet in size. To our amazement, we spotted a neat bundle of willow trail markers left by Walter Wood two years earlier. They were just peeking out of the snow right on the summit.

We again lightened our loads. We discarded the tent floor, the tent pegs, the air mattress, and some food. We were left with nineteen pounds of food to get us to Burwash Landing, which was still at least forty miles away in northeastern Canada. When we began our descent we carried about sixty pounds of equipment apiece.

None of that seemingly endless ridge was really difficult, even with our loads. But the length of it and the relentless series of drops were appalling. How anybody could have gotten up it, or even wanted to, was a mystery to both Bob and me. We saw green forests in the distance and felt sure each step brought us nearer to warmth and running water. We were rapidly getting down to God's country again.

However, it was not to be as easy as that.

On the evening of July 12, Bob and I hit the remains of Walter Woods's base camp, in a lovely location on an old flower- and grass-carpeted alluvial fan hidden behind the lateral moraine near the main bend of the Wolf Creek Glacier. We had hoped to find a huge cache of food and fuel, but found only a glass jar of peanut butter and a can of jam. Empty cans featured bear-tooth holes—the bears must have eaten everything. We hadn't completely relied on the cache, but by the time we got there we would have been very happy to sit down for a day or two and get some rest and lots more food.

We hiked down the smooth glacier for two miles, and by our reckoning were six to eight miles from the end of the ice and fifteen to twenty miles from the Donjek River. I took a small walk from our campsite and saw mountains, clearly visible beyond the Donjek, walling in our valley. Walter Wood took horses to this spot, so I thought our troubles would soon be over if we kept walking. The one thing that might prove a problem was crossing the river at that time of summer because of melting snow. In August, Walter's horses nearly drowned in it and some went in belly deep. Our only tools for raft building were a hunting knife, two packboards, and some rope, but we were certain we would find a way across.

We left camp just before 8:00 a.m. on the 13th, looking forward to reaching the end of the glacier before dusk. We found bits of horse trail, and made four miles by noon. We were weary and exhausted from a blazing sun. We got soaked crossing a large brook and then crossed three more creeks. We had been told there was a well-stocked cabin on our side of Wolf Creek, but when we found it at nearly 10:00 p.m., it was absolutely empty—it didn't even have a stove. There was no fresh water anywhere, only lots of muddy glacier melt. It was just before midnight when we reached the Donjek River and went to sleep right in the gravel, with no air mattress or anything to soften the ground.

We had four and a half days' worth of food left, and about thirty-five miles to travel to the Burwash Landing trading post. We broke camp in mid-morning, and followed an old horse trail across the gravel flats. We could not ford the river, so we gathered a little material for a raft, though soon it became apparent that a raft would be useless. The river was huge and divided into so many channels that a raft would have to be built and taken apart dozens of times to get across. Bob and I held a long conference and decided to follow the river to the end of the Donjek Glacier, probably twelve miles, cross it on the ice, and come down the other side of the valley. This was a twenty-five-mile hike to make three hundred yards of progress.

We left a cache containing my camera and film, all our extra clothing, and one packboard, high up in a tree, and took a rucksack with all of the food and one pint of gasoline. We hoped somebody would find that little cache if we died, and, by studying my pictures, at least know that we had climbed Mount Lucania. On the other packboard we loaded the tent, the one sleeping bag, our one pot, two cups, one knife, one fork, and two spoons. Then we headed upstream for the Donjek Glacier.

Late that afternoon I spotted a red squirrel in a tree. Russ Dow's pistol had rotten sights, and it took Bob four tries, but he eventually shot that squirrel. Some time later Bob told me that he had really just hit the branch from which it was watching us, and the squirrel had fallen out the tree and broken its neck when it landed! We had a lunch of squirrel soup and a handful of our last raisins.

That afternoon we finally reached the end of the Donjek Glacier, where we discovered, to our dismay, that the river did not come out of the glacier at all, and it roared in a terrible cataract between the glacier and the valley. We spent the night on the glacier, frigid cold, wrapped in our tent, which did not have a pole. (We had planned on cutting down a tree for a pole after crossing the river.) Worse, it poured all night.

The next day we reached the upper end of the Donjek Glacier and saw our river spread wide across a great gravel flat. To our distress, we now saw that it clearly originated from another glacier far up the valley. Scarcely daring to hope that we could ford the Donjek here, we set about to try, roped together with clothesline and climbing rope. It was a desperate effort to do the river piecemeal. Quicksand by the carload, a bitterly cold wind (laden with clouds of fine gray dust) blowing in our faces, and icy water added to the challenge. The Donjek River, above its glacier, was several little streams before it roared downhill to the Donjek Valley. Each time we forded a stream we felt that the next would be worse, and that we would probably have to go all the way back and on to the head of the valley, perhaps fifteen more miles.

By late morning, two channels remained—the deepest and fastest. We crossed the first beautifully, but on the second Bob went in almost to his waist. Then he hit the swift current and fell down. When he fell I was in up to my waist. He struggled to his feet, then fell again and floated downstream fast. As I braced myself to hold him, I slipped on the rocky bottom and went in, too. Thank goodness for those duffle bags, they were like huge life preservers. We sort of paddled, managed to hop and jump, and finally we both struggled, panting and half-frozen, out onto the shore. The Donjek, thank God, was behind us.

We dried our clothes and began retracing the fifteen miles along a good game trail. I was sure we would make Burwash, even if we had to do it on our hands and knees. The next day, we were making camp when a huge rabbit leapt onto the trail right in front of me. I screamed to Bob, who grabbed for the pistol and shot it. The rabbit was delicious, and the feet were our good-luck charms for the rest of the trip.

We were running low on food, but we kept making progress. On July 17 we were crossing through a bad area of tussocks and sat down, tired as hell. All of a sudden, I heard a tinkling sound like bells. Bob said, "Do you hear that funny sound?" Then Bob yelled, "By God, a pack horse." Bob saw a hat bobbing up and down and couldn't believe it. For a split second I thought he was fooling, but no: not 200 yards away, we saw first one horse, then two, then ten horses and men. We nearly went crazy with excitement. They asked where in hell we had come from, and we said we had climbed Mount Lucania and were trying to find Burwash Landing.

These men were in the employ of Gene Jacquot, who owned the Burwash Landing Trading Post. They were bringing in grub for their Donjek cabins for his fall hunting parties, and were rounding up eighteen horses who had spent the winter eating hay along the Donjek riverbed. We joined them and

Bob Bates and I walked close to ninety miles during our trek toward Burwash Landing. On July 20, we were picked up by a Pacific Alaska Airlines craft, a Lockheed Electra. Before leaving, we all paused for a photo. From left, the unnamed copilot, pilot Joe Crosson, me, Bob Bates, and Gene Jacquot, then manager of the Burwash Landing Trading Post on Kluane Lake. The post was then in the wilderness; now it's along the Alaska Highway.

got to ride horseback and gorge ourselves—I ate so much that I threw up. Bob and I slept for most of forty-eight hours while the men gathered the horses. The next morning, while I lay in a tent, Bob rode a horse across the Donjek to retrieve the film that proved we had climbed Lucania.

Bob and I reached Burwash Landing on the night of July 19. My whole body was sore from riding 30 miles on a pack saddle. Overall, not counting doubling back and hauling loads, I estimated we walked 86½ miles and covered 116 miles overland. When we got back to Alaska, I sent a dispatch to the *New York Herald–Tribune*. With a dateline of Valdez, I told the story of the climb. It ran under the headline "First Man to Scale Mt. Lucania Describes 17,150-foot Ice Peak" with a photograph of Bob.

When I got home I told *Life* magazine the story of the climb and they bought my pictures for a thousand bucks—in those days, that was an awful pile of money. In September, *Life* ran a story written by another reporter, accompanying my pictures about the first ascent of Lucania. When Walter Wood had climbed Steele, he had written a story for *Life*, and at the end had stated that Lucania was unclimbable. I wanted to prove him wrong, and we did.

Later I learned that Bob Reeve, apparently trying to be reassuring, had sent a letter to my mother, dated July 9, indicating that all was well with Bob Bates and me (even though he had absolutely no way of knowing if we were alive or dead). "Please don't worry about the boys," he wrote, "for in spite of the remoteness of their whereabouts I am sure that everything is going to be OK. Nine-tenths of their battle was over when they landed on Walsh Glacier."

At no time during our ordeal did Bob and I really doubt that we would be able to get out of the backcountry wilderness. We were overconfident, if anything—we didn't look ahead. If we had known what we would have to do to get out of it, we would probably have thought we were been better off committing suicide. But we took it day by day. As Bob Reeve used to say, "Skin one skunk at a time. Don't go down the hole looking for another one."

CHAPTER TEN

MORE NEW ROUTES IN ALASKA

By 1938 I really felt that Alaska was the place to be. I could climb high mountains no one else had climbed, explore new territory, and have fun, too. That summer I was part of the first ascents of Mount Marcus Baker (at 13,250 feet, the tallest mountain in the Chugach Range), and Mount Sanford in the Wrangell–St. Elias Mountains (at 16,200 feet, then the tallest unclimbed mountain in North America).

Marcus Baker was a horrible trip. I was with Norman Dyhrenfurth, who later helped organize the first American ascent of Mount Everest; Norman Bright, who had climbed with me before; and Peter Gabriel, an excellent Swiss-German climber. We were flown in to the mountain from Valdez by Bob Reeve, and approached the mountain from a landing on the Matanuska Glacier.

Most Alaskans are familiar with the Chugach Mountain range because it is the eastern horizon of Anchorage. Many people climb the small mountains, 3,000–4,000 feet high, that are right next to the city. Marcus Baker is nowhere near there, and typically has much worse weather than these smaller peaks (like Mount Flattop, which everybody climbs on the summer solstice).

We started on a big bend of the Matanuska Glacier, perhaps seventy driving miles from Anchorage along the Glenn Highway. Again, the airplane made a big difference for us: we didn't have to lug huge amounts of supplies overland, or walk miles to reach a good starting place on the route. We started in May and were there well into June, and it snowed every day on that trip. It was perfectly terrible. We climbed for ten days and it snowed all the time. It should not have been a long siege on the mountain, an expedition like an Everest—and in fact we did 90 percent of the climbing in three days, but the snow made it rough. Most of the time we were just sitting out the snowfall.

The main reason to go to Marcus Baker was to be able to say that we had climbed the highest mountain in the Chugach Range. At the time I was interested in climbing the key peaks in Alaska. Marcus Baker is an easy climb, but any time you go near Prince William Sound you are asking for weather trouble. It rained and rained while we were sorting and packing our supplies, before we got to the glacier, and then it snowed and snowed while we were there. This is an area the sun forgot; as I look back at my diary entries from mid-May, most of them begin, "Rain." On May 22, when we flew in four loads of equipment, I concluded my comments with, "Pouring rain all day."

When it was time to set up our Marcus Baker base camp, the real question was whether the clouds would let us land. We circled in Bob Reeve's plane for ten minutes at the head of the Valdez Glacier, and suddenly came out at 8,000 feet in beautiful sunshine. Still, a queer haze hid Marcus Baker and everything to the southwest of it was very forbidding. It was a warning of an approaching storm. Many more followed.

Some days we made no progress at all, and other days it felt as if we were never going to make any progress. By June 16

In 1938, I made a first ascent of Mount Sanford, among other peaks. This photo shows Jack Kennedy, horse packer and wilderness guide, near 16,000-foot Mount Sanford one late afternoon.

we were at Camp V at 9,000 feet, on the snow shoulder of the northwest ridge. Climbing up to put in Camp VI at 9,800 feet, I could see only to the next willow-wand marker, one hundred or so feet ahead, because of the fog. But it was also warm, reaching 60 degrees. So I was astounded when it began to snow. We still made a thousand feet an hour in our ascent with loads of sixty pounds, so I thought we were getting into pretty fine shape.

What a night we had on June 17! It was blowing like fury. The temperature was 20 degrees and nowhere but in a sleeping bag felt at all pleasant. The wind velocity got higher and higher, and more and more gusty. At 9:30 P.M., the tent was roaring and flapping and snapping so hard that we pulled down the pole and wrapped ourselves in it.

Then a real nightmare started. With the pole down, the guy ropes and pegs held the tent partly up. The cloth began flapping and snapping around like crazy, tossing food and clothing and pots all over the place. The whole inside of the tent was coated with a thin veneer of ice from the steam of supper. This kept breaking off all over us, which made things doubly disgusting. Norman and I thought we had it under control, but when we went back to bed we were almost knocked out by the tent whipping up and down on our heads. We weighted it down with boots and made a barricade of our clothes. You might as well have tried to sleep beside a riveting machine. Several times during the night we had to get up and shake piles of snow off our heads, or we would have been buried completely.

The next morning the tent was perfect chaos. One of our Primus stoves was upside down in a pool of gasoline. The big water pail was right-side up, but one of the tent door ropes had fallen into it and was frozen in so hard we had to cut it out. Everything else—food, clothes, and pots—was in the wildest conceivable confusion—a hopeless mess. The speed of the previous night's gusts must have been 60 mph. The whole storm had come and gone without a change in the barometer. Never in my life did I expect to see a more terrible neck of the woods for weather.

The next day Norman Bright and I made a two-hour reconnaissance to the 11,000-foot col. The going was perfect, hard-packed crust with about two or three inches of soft powder on top. We weaved back and forth among the cracks in the most abominable weather conditions: no wind, but thick fog. The sun burned through at intervals, giving us a slight idea of our direction.

We discussed over and over what to do next. The conditions were so formidable that we considered breaking camp and heading down to Valdez. After another unholy night, we rose at 5:30 A.M. on June 19. Then we felt a slight letup in the wind and had a glorious sunrise. The valley below was clear for the first time in days. Our trail from the recon was blown over in many places, but was still visible because of the willow markers. We decided to go for it.

We left camp at 9:00 A.M. At the start, Peter Gabriel led for two hours of laborious trailbreaking, to the col between the two unnamed 12,000-foot peaks. The whole west was a sea of rich black clouds and rain squalls. To the east, all was blue over a sea of white clouds. Looking out, I realized that there had to be nearly a dozen or more unmapped 10,000-foot mountains in this part of the range, stretching from our camp westward to Palmer.

The weather was good enough to justify going a bit further. We passed over the second unnamed peak. Our hopes of mapping and taking pictures were pretty much extinguished because of the fog. We thought that two storms fighting against each other from opposite sides of the range might jointly give us a sporting chance at the great prize of Marcus Baker, which towered between the other peaks. It took just one minute to decide to keep going. We had plenty of food and plenty of clothes, and the success of the expedition was at stake.

We kept on and Norman Bright and Peter placed a steady trail of willow wands for our retreat. Without a good supply we would never have dared to try the climb. The snow was drifting so hard that fifteen minutes after we passed, our trail was entirely gone—except for a friendly line of willow wands staked upright in the wind-scoured surface.

Nearing 1:30 P.M., we took off our crampons, cursed that we had left our snowshoes below, and started up the long grind of the final plateau, breaking knee deep through the wind-blown crust at every step. The fog rose and fell, every once in a while allowing us a glimpse of our direction. The sun boiling down through the fog was terrific, but it was so cold that your fingers got numb the second you took off your gloves. Shortly before 3:00 P.M., from the shoulder, we saw Marcus Baker rising steel-gray a mile or so ahead of us, just a little mist obscuring its peak. The weather threatened, but no worse than before.

The slope falling into the col from our side was very steep and icy at the start, so we speedily put on our crampons again. Then we hit a stretch of fathomless, ice-cold flour. A little later, leading waist deep in this horrible stuff got so tiring that we stopped in the bottom of a hollow about three-quarters of a mile from the summit, now completely lost in clouds.

We nibbled some prunes, dates, and cookies, but it was so bitterly cold we didn't dare linger any longer than absolutely necessary. All afternoon, we had two thoughts: Can we climb Marcus Baker? And can we fight our way back up those 12,000-foot peaks that lay between us and camp? We put on extra clothing and started our last assault at 3:30 by what seemed to be the speediest route to the top.

Peter and I took turns leading in the terrific snow; then it turned hard and icy and we put on crampons again. The mist hung almost steadily over the top. We made our way over two large crevasses and started zigzagging up the final ridge. The fog was so thick that we made the last half hour only by dead reckoning.

When we reached the summit dome we didn't even know we were on the top, because of the fog. Snow showers and fog wiped out visibility, though we felt sure of where we had to go. I got one of the guys to put his ice axe into a hole, and I went around in a circle with a hundred feet of rope tied to me. When I realized that it was downhill in every direction, we figured that had to be the top. Norman Bright and I let out a triumphant yell and the others followed three minutes behind, their black figures materializing mysteriously out of the mist. We spent ten minutes on top of that miserable mountain, and then we said, "Let's get the hell out of here."

Usually, a mountain climber will take the time to enjoy the view from the top. We never got any view at all. I always wanted to go back near the top of Marcus Baker in a helicopter, because the view from the top, with all of those mountains spread out beneath it on a clear day, must be gorgeous.

We had gone over two unnamed peaks more than 12,000 feet high, and down the other side of each to get there. Then we climbed back over them to get home. The weather was mighty poor all the way, and we didn't reach camp until thirteen hours after our departure. It was as tough a day as you could possibly expect.

After the Marcus Baker expedition, I went on to Mount Sanford. This was a pleasurable trip with my friend Terris Moore and his wife, Katrina, who went up to 10,000 feet. Sanford is a gorgeous sight—more than 16,000 feet high, it's just a big, gentle snow slope on the side we chose to climb. It was the highest unclimbed mountain in Alaska, and Terry and I thought it would be great fun to climb it on skis and have a good ski run on the way down.

The approach to this Alaskan mountain was quite different from what I was used to: we began in an automobile right off the Richardson Highway. But the funny thing was that it was just as foggy as it had been on Marcus Baker. Terry was driving like a railroad engineer, with his head out the window. We were supposed to have a truck, but the man with whom we had made the arrangements had never turned up. We ended up using a station wagon, loaded to the gills—we must have had fifteen hundred pounds of gear in it. We took out the backseat, and we carried everything from bananas to a briefcase.

As we headed toward Gulkana, we hit a bump and had a terrific blowout. The load was just too much for the rear tires, and one just exploded with a horrible roar. It took forty-five minutes to get it fixed. Luckily, we carried two extra tires.

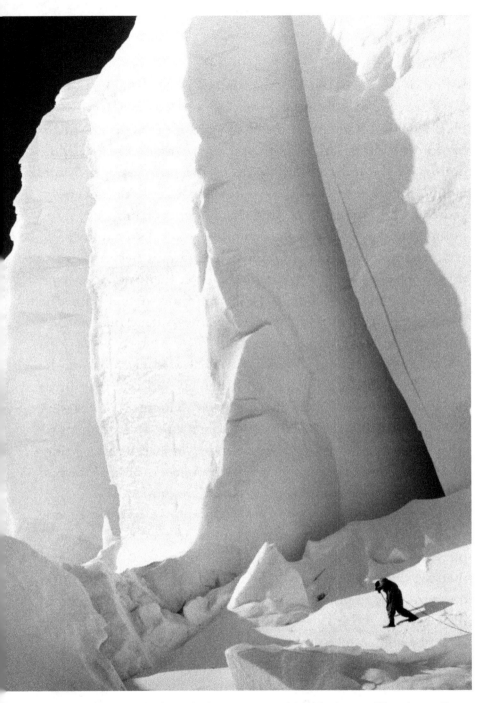

Norman Bright at the foot of a huge snow-and-ice block near Silverthrone Pass, 1945.

As we drove along, the Wrangell Range came into view, just before we reached Gakona. The whole Copper River was spread out before us, with its myriad channels and bars and great gravel bluffs. Behind it stretched the beautiful Alpine tableland that is Sanford's lava plateau, smooth and unbroken all the way to the bottom of the mountain. The tip of the peak was just visible, riding like an ivory ship above a towering sea of thunderheads gathered about its base. Mount Drum was beautiful, too, more pointed, and a good four thousand feet lower than Sanford.

There are a few well-populated communities in the area now, and when the sun is out, people get thrilling views from the Glenn Highway. But in 1938 there was virtually no one there except a small population of Native Americans, maybe a trapper or two, and no tourists at all.

Mount Sanford, however, is not located right beside the road. We parked, unloaded, and then packed our gear in by horseback, making camps along the way. The mosquitoes were fantastic in that swampy land, not something we had encountered in any of our other Alaska climbs. We had hired a guide, who, with several packhorses, got us to the beginning of the real climb. (His name, of all things, was Adam Sanford.)

When we got closer to the mountain, we transferred our equipment to a hired dog team and the dogs mushed our supplies to higher elevations. We had a camp at 10,000 feet, and then the dogs got up to more than 12,000 feet. By that elevation it was snowing to beat the band. The dogs got all buggered up in their harness and it slowed things down. At first, we thought we might be able to take the dogs all the way to the summit, but we ended up using them only to haul supplies to our final camp.

On July 21 it was snowing as hard in the morning as it had been the night before. The sun appeared every so often, but it seemed a long way off. It was amazingly warm at our 10,000-

At the end of a busy summer, in September 1938, pilot Merritt Kirkpatrick and I lined up some of my equipment for a photo in front of his Bellanca Skyrocket at Cordova. Shown here is my fifty-three-pound Fairchild K-6 aerial camera and my Fairchild K-3B, which I used for vertical mapping photographs. On top of the K-3B is my DeVry 35 mm moving-picture camera. And in the foreground are a couple of oxygen tanks, used while flying above 15,000 feet.

foot camp, but it was still storming. I was planning to hunker down with a magazine when the weather suddenly cleared. The sun came out in boiling fashion at noon, and we made the determination that it was more than a local clear-off. The signs were good enough to push Terry and me out of camp at 1:30 P.M. after hastily organizing our two light loads of equipment.

The first few willow wands we had previously placed were buried in fresh snow. Sanford rose before us magnificently clear at the head of its tremendous snow slope, a tiny white cloud nestled to the west of its top. A cool, northeast breeze kept the snow a fine powder under our skis. The ascent of Sanford was turning out to be the same as the ascents of Crillon and Marcus Baker—a race with the weather. But skis were very, very different from snowshoes.

We reached the top of the first rise, 10,800 feet, at 2:10, and the second snow dome, 11,300 feet, at 2:40. A good solid pace of a thousand feet per hour. We had been wearing white shirts over our flannel underwear until then, when we added flannel shirts. A slight northerly breeze was pretty cool. We passed 12,000 feet at 3:45, and then fought deep powder snow, nearly knee-deep on skis, across two upper crevasses. The summit was still wonderfully clear with deep blue sky behind it, but huge masses of black clouds to the north were slowly creeping toward us, casting a black shadow over the solid cumulus ceiling below them.

Terry and I took turns at the lead, until we were too tired to proceed without a rest. At 6:30 we reached 14,500 feet and a cache of trail markers we had left behind on the 19th. We had had gone 4,500 feet in five hours, breaking trail all the way, with only two ten-minute rests. The weather was still ominous. The big black storm slowly approached and cast its evil shadow on us. We were getting much colder, and our ski boots were beginning to freeze. An hour later the summit seemed just as far ahead as before, and we shifted the lead constantly. Just below the summit, right in the middle of the steepest, most slippery part, Terry's left sealskin came off. There was no time to lose. I swung up into the lead and by the time the rope between us was tight again, he was ready to move ahead once more.

The mist blew away and we saw ahead of us what seemed to be a low, snow-filled bowl. Was this the crater that we thought we might find on top of Sanford from the aerial photographs that I had made? Would we have to go down inside a crater and climb back out before we could reach the top? That would be too wicked of the mountain. I turned our route to the left a bit, and the crater became a small hollow. Surely the top was just ahead.

At 9:00 P.M., Terry halted just ahead of me, and I joined him on the very top of Sanford. A grand handshake and a big slap on the back for each of us followed a happy yell of conquest. We spent twenty-five wonderful minutes on top. Fourteen-thousand-foot Mount Wrangell was way below us, its many snowy summits contrasting magnificently with the deep evening shadows at the head of the great basin of the Copper Glacier.

We had forged all the way to the top in one push, on skis with sealskins, in seven and a half hours. We took in the gorgeous views, too briefly, then it fogged in on our way back down and we needed to follow our trail markers to guard against getting lost. We descended in wide zigzags from one side of the trail to the other, our eyes constantly peeled for crevasses. We did not get back to camp until 10:45 P.M., but that was fine given the abundant summer light.

Two great climbing triumphs in the same season! And before I left Alaska that summer of 1938, I completed more National Geographic photographic flights over the St. Elias Range. Alaska was definitely a place I loved to be.

CHAPTER ELEVEN

A CAREER AND A MARRIAGE ARE BORN

Late in 1938, still working at Harvard, I took a trip to Philadelphia to make a speech on the first ascent of Mount Lucania at the opening of the new Hall of Earth History at the Philadelphia Academy of Science. It was November 17, and sitting on the plane I noticed a familiar bald spot on the head of a man a few rows ahead of me.

I moved up and sat next to John K. Howard, a Massachusetts attorney, who proceeded to tell me that he had been elected president of a museum in Boston called the New England Museum of Natural History, and that it had a dreadful director whose only interest was studying minerals. Howard explained that he was having a heck of a time finding a young new director who could take on the old museum and make something new of it. Founded in 1864, it was the second-oldest natural history museum in the United States; only the one in Charleston, South Carolina, was older. Yet he had been turned down by two good candidates for the job.

Then he asked what I was doing. I told him I was the assistant director of the Harvard Institute of Geographical Exploration, but that I felt the Harvard Geology Department was successfully trying to manage the collapse of the Institute.

All of a sudden, Howard said, "You're exactly the fellow I'm looking for!" However, we were already descending into Newark, where he was getting off, and we had no time to pursue the matter further. I flew on to Philadelphia to give my lecture.

At this time, I was trying to figure out just what my next step in life would be. I was twenty-eight years old and looking to make a professional move, so John Howard's words gave me something to think about. He didn't give me much time to think them over, though. That night, just as I was about to be introduced to the audience by Charlie Cadwalader, the president of the Philadelphia Academy, he reached into his pocket and gave me a telegram from Howard, sent from New York.

It said, "I meant what I said on the airplane this morning. I want you to accept the position of Director of the New England Museum of Natural History. See you as soon as we return to Boston."

Shortly thereafter, I dined with Howard and two of his most important and persuasive trustees, Ludlow Griscom, of Harvard's Museum of Comparative Zoology, and Wendell Endicott, a very wealthy gentleman and president of the Boston opera. I told them I didn't have the slightest idea about how to run a museum, nor did I have any experience in fund-raising—and it was clear a lot of fund-raising lay ahead. They wanted the new director to preside over significant changes in the operation, as well as a move to another location (it was perfectly obvious that the current location, in the middle of downtown, would be overwhelmed by a major parking problem if the museum began to attract large crowds).

I could see that they would have to raise a lot of money, and I brought this up. They said, "We'll raise the money. Your job will be to have the ideas which will make all of this possible." They finally convinced me that I should take the job.

I was elected director at the trustees' meeting of December 28, 1938, and went to work at the museum beginning March 1, 1939. I stayed on as director until 1980, and kept an office at the new Boston Museum of Science as director emeritus for more than twenty additional years. As for John Howard's promise that I would not be responsible for the fund-raising, I ended up doing almost nothing but raising money for four decades. During my forty-one years as director I helped raise $216 million for the museum. When I took over the New England Museum of Natural History, its annual budget was $44,000 and it attracted 40,000 people a year with no admission fee. Six decades later, the Museum of Science's annual budget was $31.6 million and it attracted 1.6 million visitors a year.

Simply getting the land to expand the museum was a helluva process. We had to go through the state legislature and various committees. We had just one acre of property downtown for the old museum; the new museum today occupies 5.6 acres.

At the time, the question was where to put it. I was still going all over the place to give presentations about climbing mountains in Alaska. Each invitation gave me the opportunity to talk as the director of a barely existent institution. One day, I was returning from a trip to New York, where I had given yet another lecture about Alaska. Decades ago, airplanes only landed into the wind—if there was a bad crosswind, they switched runways. There was a big east wind that day, so we came in for a landing over East Cambridge; I was sitting on the right side of the plane and looking out the window. That turned out to be very good luck, because I saw an area that intrigued me. I checked into real estate availability and was told it was a great patch of land, more than five acres, owned by the state. We had to go to the legislature to lease it. Bill Morrissey, for whom they named Morrissey Boulevard, and who ran the metropolitan District Commission at the time, helped me a lot.

After the final vote, one of the committee members who had voted in my favor put his hand on my shoulder as we walked out of the room in the State House and said, "Young man, you've got what you wanted. Now, why the hell do you want to build that museum looking out over the Boston and Maine freight yards?" I said, "We're going to look in the other direction!" Which meant looking at the whole Charles River Basin— it's an absolutely gorgeous view.

I began work at the old museum and the trustees gave me a perfectly awful secretary. She was determined to do everything she could to put her foot in front of me so that I would trip, because the last thing she wanted was for the museum to move, or be run by a new director. Finally, I said, "I refuse to go further with this thing unless you get me a new secretary."

Very soon I began the search for a new secretary. I put out the word everywhere—I even told Clarkie, the mailman who serviced the Harvard Biology Laboratories and the Institute of Geographical Exploration. He passed the information on to a young woman in the Harvard biology lab named Barbara Teel Polk. Clarkie described me, and told her, "This is an interesting opportunity for you." Her first reaction was, "I want no part of working for a crazy mountain climber, or in that dusty old museum." (Barbara's theory was that anyone who climbed mountains must be nuts.)

Ultimately, under pressure from Clarkie, she agreed to an interview with me in the old museum building, and she was not impressed at all. She said the place was musty, and later said she had had no intention of taking a job there. But I didn't want to let her get away; I told her to think it over and I would telephone her.

The Polk family portrait includes, from left, Barbara, at about age six; her brother, Alvar "Jim" Polk, Jr.; mother, Maybell Teel Polk; father, Alvar W. Polk; and sister, Edith Polk.

According to Barbara, I called her for about ten evenings in succession. Finally, she decided, "If this guy is so aggressive, this museum might succeed, and it could prove to be a very interesting job." I was just desperate to get a good secretary quickly. If we developed feelings for one another beyond the professional, they went unspoken.

Some time later, I was headed to give a lecture on my ascent of Mount Lucania at the Travelers Insurance Company in Hartford, Connecticut. I brought my own projectionist with me, because the success of the lecture depended entirely on the projection of the pictures. A janitor at the museum named John McCormick (whom we called Mac) handled my slide projection.

That day Barbara came into the museum dressed a little bit better than usual and Mac said, "Why are you so dressy today?" Barbara said, "I'm going down to New York to spend the weekend with a boyfriend of mine." So Mac said, "Why don't you drive with me as far as Hartford, and then take the night train to New York?" When they got to Hartford, he pointed out that she had hours to wait before the train and she might as well come see the show. "You've never seen your boss's pictures." I didn't know she was coming, and at the end of the lecture I spied her in the audience.

I said, "My God, what are you doing down here?" She said she had to catch the midnight train for a weekend date in New York. Barbara didn't have a berth and was just going to sit in a coach car. I was going to New York to give another lecture—"Hell," I said, "I'll give you my berth and I'll take the upper berth." She agreed. After we both got into bed and said good-night, I reached my hand down. Barbara has always said she didn't know quite whether to pretend that she didn't see it. Instead, she raised her hand up and I gave it a little squeeze. I was starting to think of her as an attractive woman, not just a secretary.

The next morning, when we arrived at the station in New York, I said, "I'm going to have breakfast with Lowell Thomas. Why don't you come and have breakfast with us?" Lowell Thomas was already a big shot on the radio and as a writer. We had a pleasant time—only later did we learn that Lowell went

home and told his wife, "I just met Brad Washburn's future wife." He somehow knew it, though neither of us did at that point. Later on, Lowell said, "I saw it in all four of your eyes."

After breakfast, Barbara went her way and I went to give my lecture. The next day, I was taking the afternoon train back to Boston and there she was on the platform, waiting for the same train. We sat together and spent the four hours chatting all the way home. In a sense, this was our first chance to be together just as two people, not a boss and a secretary.

The next day at the office, Barbara said something seemed new and different about me. I drove her home from work, and that evening at her house I spontaneously asked her to marry me—and she said, "I accept." She also said a little later, "I haven't the slightest idea why I accepted."

It was that fast, but we had sensed something. We hadn't even gone out on a date, yet I didn't have to agonize over asking her for her hand in marriage. We really did no thinking. I just asked, and she just answered. It's the best decision I ever made.

If not for having seen the back of John Howard's head, and moving up in the airplane cabin, I doubt whether I would ever have had anything to do with the Museum of Science. There might not even have been a Museum of Science. Nor would I have met Barbara. That was a real turning point in my life.

Barbara and I were married on April 27, 1940, and celebrated our sixty-fourth wedding anniversary on April 27, 2004.

Barbara and I were married on April 27, 1940.

We took six other fellows along on our "honeymoon" trip—the first ascent of 10,180-foot Mount Bertha. Our little expedition included, back row, from left: Lee Wilson, Alva Morrison, Michl Feuersinger, and Lowell Thomas, Jr. In front, from left, Maynard Miller, me, Barbara, and Tom Winship. The photo was taken July 31, 1940, about three months after our wedding.

CHAPTER TWELVE

BARBARA CLIMBS
HER FIRST MOUNTAIN

In the summer of 1940, I planned to return to Alaska to climb Mount Bertha. I was fascinated by this 10,182-foot peak for a couple of reasons: it was an unclimbed peak in the same region as Mount Fairweather and Mount Crillon, and it would give me an opportunity to take my new wife to Alaska to climb on an expedition that wasn't too difficult.

Barbara and I were married at the end of April, and we left for Alaska in June. We had not talked about mountain climbing before we were married, and Barbara had never climbed a mountain, but I was sure she could do it. Throughout the spring I made plans for the expedition and I always planned for her to go, but she said later that I never actually asked her, that she overheard me making all of these plans and had no idea if she was to be included or not. Then she heard me mention her name on the list of people on the expedition, and realized that I was counting on her to be there and to climb to the top.

After our wedding, Barbara and I went on a ski trip in the Mount Washington area of New Hampshire for a brief honeymoon, but later, when I was lecturing, I called the Mount Bertha trip our "Alaskan honeymoon."

I didn't expect this climb to be that challenging. We were joined on the trip by young Lowell Thomas, Jr., who was a teenager, and Tom Winship, who later became the distinguished editor of the *Boston Globe*. Barbara was the only girl, and I assumed there would be no problems about that—everyone got along with Barbara. However, she did say later in her diary that she was very concerned about being the only woman on the journey, and wanted to make a good showing. She didn't want any of the guys to say that the only reason she came along was because she was my wife.

Our preparations were hectic right up until our June 20 departure from Boston. When we got on the train—we took the Canadian National Railway to Prince Rupert, British Columbia—we were seen off by family and friends, who took pictures and wished us a good journey. We had six dogs with us for this trip. (We borrowed them from Norman Vaughan, who had dropped out of Harvard to travel with Admiral Richard Byrd to Antarctica in 1928 as a dog handler, and who later moved to Alaska and competed in the Iditarod Trail Sled Dog Race in his seventies.) The dogs got into fights in the baggage car more than once; later, taxi drivers wouldn't give us a ride between trains because of all the gear and the dogs. Then, on the way, my hay fever reared up in the Canadian Rockies and I caught a cold.

Finally, we took a boat from the Pacific Northwest to Alaska, sailing on the S.S. *Prince George* through Ketchikan, where we saw Bob Ellis, my old pilot, and on to Juneau, where we lunched with Territorial Governor Ernest Gruening. We switched to a smaller boat and headed to Glacier Bay, and then on to Hugh Miller Inlet.

When we disembarked we went up the Hugh Miller Glacier—which has since totally melted away—to the head of a

Climbing Mount Bertha in 1940, Barbara helped transport a 200-pound load of gasoline and tools for Camp III on the Brady Glacier.

valley. We came out on a huge plateau called the Brady Ice Field. We drove our dog team across the ice field to the bottom of Mount Bertha. That put us on the interior side of the Fairweather Range, away from the Gulf of Alaska. (Today, to get to a place like that, all guides need do is hire an airplane with ski wheels. A flight of less than an hour from Juneau will drop you off next to the mountain.)

This area is very close to the international boundary between Alaska and Canada. At the time we had no idea how Mount Bertha was named, and I didn't learn what was behind the name for many years. It turns out that the International

Boundary Commission had a large number of men working on the surveying project and Bertha was a prostitute in Skagway who gave great happiness to the workers, gaining a certain measure of fame for her efforts.

In 1940, it was very rare for a woman to be included on an expedition. Some women had made early climbs in Alaska; Mount Blackburn, I believe, was climbed by Dora Keen Handy. But for a woman to be invited on an otherwise all-men's expedition was very rare. The other members of the expedition knew before we left that she was going, and they had to accept her or not make the trip. Lowell Thomas, Jr., was only sixteen years old; his father wanted him to go, and figured that if Barbara was going it must be easy. When we started up the lower ridge of Bertha, Lowell followed at the back for a while before returning to camp. He said to Barbara, "Is your husband trying to kill you right off?" Lowell never did become a mountain climber, but he became a wonderful Bush pilot in Alaska.

Tom Winship was then the president of the Harvard ski team. I wanted to get some skiing pictures, which would help me in my lecturing, which would in turn generate income to pay the bills for the trip. For Tom, the trip was mostly a summer vacation. I had just turned thirty and Tom turned twenty on the trip—we put twenty candles on a piece of board to celebrate his birthday. There were eight of us altogether; the others were Alva Morrison, Maynard Miller, Michl Feuersinger, and Lee Wilson.

We were at base camp on July 2 when Barbara got her first experience walking on a glacier and jumping over a crevasse. She said, "It wasn't half bad." On July 4, I woke the group by firing two shots of a pistol as an alarm clock. Happy Independence Day!

On July 21, we set up an advanced base camp under the

ridge of Bertha, then I walked a short way up with Barbara and Michl and took some movies. On a cloudy July 25, I took some

---

While at the base camp for the Mount Bertha climb in 1940, I had a major crisis. I had my huge Fairchild K-6 aerial camera with me, and I was taking a few close-up pictures of the party on the ground. When I wound up the shutter curtain there was a horrible noise. And then the shutter refused to work at all. I hadn't yet taken any aerial pictures, and there was no lab within a thousand miles that could fix that camera. The pressure was on me to fix it by myself. How on earth could I do it with only pliers, a file, a hammer, some copper wire, and a screwdriver?

I took apart the whole focal plane shutter assembly— which I had never done before—using only those tools, where- upon I discovered that a tiny metal bolt, at the heart of the shutter, was sheared in two. This seemed to be next to impos- sible to fix, but somehow, I just plain had to fix that camera. A large part of the income intended to finance most of the trip was expected to come from the sale of my aerial photographs.

In the first-aid kit, I found a blanket pin intended for use with a sling. So I patiently began to file down the thick- ness of the blanket pin until it seemed to be the exact thickness of the shutter pin. After a couple of hours of work I had shaped the new pin perfectly to fit into the tiny hole. That was a victory, but I still had to tighten the spring that controlled the speed of the shutter curtain. I had taken hundreds of pic- tures with that camera, and I thought I might be able to guess the speed of the shutter by the kind of bang it made when I pressed the trigger.

Over and over again we tightened that spring, until I thought I heard the kind of bang I usually heard each time I took a picture. Then, putting my trust in God, I took 242 aerial photographs over the next month. When we at last reached home at the end of the summer, I got the shutter assembly examined at Kodak's research laboratory in Rochester, New York. They told me that instead of the 1/225th of a second the camera was originally set for, I had taken my pictures at 1/215th of a second. Wow. That's about as close as you can get by feel.

---

pictures of Barbara in her sleeping bag; then, when it cleared in the afternoon, Maynard, Tom, Michl, Barbara, and I put in a new, higher camp.

The next day we began moving up the ridge. Barbara was roped to me. There were some knife-edged areas, but I stopped frequently to take pictures. She said later that those stops gave her some scraps of needed rest. Once, Barbara slid on the ice and banged her elbow on some rocks; she rappelled over one difficult spot and ended up dangling on the rope in mid-air, because she couldn't get a grip on the icy slope. She was laughing, so I didn't think much of it, but she had been very scared.

We took some rest days, during which we had some thick fog, but on July 30 it seemed as if the clouds might clear. We got started about 5:00 A.M. and after a rushed breakfast, I yelled, "Let's go!"

It was a lot of work over snow, an uphill rock climb, and down into a narrow pass. The sky cleared after we passed our

At the summit of Mount Bertha with Barbara, 3:30 P.M. At front, from left, is Maynard Miller, Michl Feuersinger, and Thomas Winship.

previously placed cache at 8:00, and from then on the views were terrific. We looked over at Mount Crillon, and saw the top of Fairweather in the distance. After many hours, the final cone of Bertha at last came into view, and the last half hour of climbing was through deep snow.

On Bertha's summit, the group raised the American flag and the banner of the National Geographic Society. Barbara and I stood happily on the summit together. That was an exciting moment. And Tom Winship snapped a photograph that is the best picture ever taken of Barbara and me together. (Later, when I was retiring as the museum's director, famed painter

Barbara on the summit of her first Alaska mountain, Mount Bertha, in 1940.

Bill Draper made a portrait of us from that photo. The painting hangs in the museum lobby today.)

We had reached the summit of Mount Bertha at 3:30 in the afternoon, and had spent considerable time taking pictures. I expected to take about six hours to return to camp; the going was rougher than we thought it would be, however, and it took nineteen hours and forty minutes in all to make the exhausting round-trip.

Barbara acquitted herself superbly on the first ascent of Mount Bertha—as I had known she would. I never at any moment worried about her. It was the beginning of a marvelous partnership in the field, and in marriage. She accompanied me on so many of my other trips to Alaska. She's been wonderful. She's been everything to me.

Our first child, Dorothy (or "Dotty"), was born on March 7, 1941. Here we are, celebrating her first Christmas, in our tiny apartment at 180 Commonwealth Avenue, Boston.

CHAPTER THIRTEEN

BLENDING FAMILY AND ALASKA

On March 7, 1941, our daughter Dorothy Polk Washburn was born. Up until Barbara became pregnant we had never talked about having a family, never assumed we'd have children. Neither of us talked about it. When we had Dorothy, we began to talk about it. (Our son, Edward Hall Washburn, whom we call Ted, was born on September 25, 1942. And our second daughter, Elizabeth Bradford Washburn, whom we call Betsy, was born on June 21, 1946.)

Far from raising a family of mountaineers—not something that entered my mind, anyway—our kids have not been interested in mountains. When Barbara and I were away from home when they were growing up, it was because we were involved with mountains, primarily in Alaska. I think the kids were not interested in the mountains because they saw them as rivals. I can't say that I am disappointed that none of them showed an interest in the mountains—I was never interested in anyone following in my footsteps.

Our children did their own things, and I think they were happy we didn't push them into anything. Barbara and I did everything we could to reinforce their interests and enthusiasm. For instance, Ted was a coxswain in rowing, and he is one

Our baby was six months old when Barbara joined me on the first ascent of the 13,740-foot-high Mount Hayes, in Alaska's Interior.

of the best crew coaches in the world. He was involved with Harvard and the University of California, though his main job today is running the Boston office of recording for the blind. Dorothy worked as the secretary for a prominent Boston surgeon and then became a homemaker. Betsy, who worked at Harvard in the design office, later became a teacher in Colorado. She has a son, who is interested in the mountains—he goes to college near Seattle, and has shown some real interest in climbing and hiking. The other eight grandchildren are just not interested at all. One of the boys may make a good diplomat—he's in China, and he speaks pretty fluent Chinese.

Later in 1941, the year after we made the first ascent of Mount Bertha, Barbara joined me on the first ascent of Mount Hayes in Alaska. Hayes is 13,740 feet high and is located ninety miles southeast of Fairbanks in the Alaskan Interior. It's nowhere near the other mountains I had been climbing in Southeast Alaska.

I had thought Bertha was a rather dull climb. Mount Hayes is steep and has terrific exposure; I thought it would be a much better climb for Barbara. The only attempt on the mountain had failed at 9,000 feet, but I knew from looking at it from the air that it had to be climbable. It was spectacular and much more difficult than Bertha.

Our climb of Mount Hayes was the only trip I ever made to climb a virgin peak in Alaska that did not have a scientific or photographic objective (though we did get some good movies that later produced income for the family). I was motivated to make the first ascent because it was apparent to us by that summer that the war raging in Europe was probably going to spread, and go on for quite some time. I thought that years might pass before another good ascent could be made in Alaska.

My friend Henry Hall was supposed to have joined us on Mount Marcus Baker in 1938, and had cancelled his involvement because of the death of his son. Henry studied the reasons for the failure of the 1937 attempt on Hayes, and his enthusiasm and financial support pushed us into giving it a try. All of the others in the party, except Barbara, expected to be drafted in the near future, and we thought we might not get another climbing chance for a long time.

The expedition to Mount Hayes began on June 25, and Barbara and I were joined by Henry Hall, Sterling Hendricks, Benjamin Ferris, and William Shand. Once again Barbara and I boarded a train west and then a boat north. (Our daughter Dorothy joined my mother and father at Squam Lake.) We learned that Bob Ellis had been called up by the Navy, to serve out of Sitka, and he and his family had moved there. When we

Climbing together with heavy loads, here we are at 8,000 feet on the ridge of Mount Hayes during its first ascent. The summit was reached at 1:45 P.M. on August 11, 1941. This was my only climb to a virgin peak in Alaska that did not have a scientific or photographic objective.

checked a newspaper in early July we read that Adolph Hitler was raising hell in Russia and that the German and Russian navies were fighting in the Baltic Sea. It was incongruous reading after a glorious trip through the Wrangell Narrows at sunset: we saw a fawn by the water's side, and a large bald eagle gliding between the tips of two tall, dark spruce trees. We caught glimpses of Fairweather and Crillon above the clouds, and then we pushed on through Cordova to Valdez. It was great fun showing the town to Barbara.

We loaded our 1,700 pounds of freight on top of 9,600 bottles of beer for the 371-mile truck haul to Fairbanks. Then, on July 10, we flew to Hayes beneath fast-gathering clouds and showers. We arrived safely on a 1,200-foot miners' landing strip, cut barely as wide as the span of the plane's wings, and trimmed through the low branches of a flattened gravel bar.

When we flew back to Fairbanks after making a neat cache, we circled the lower part of Mount Hayes and very clearly saw its glaciers and ridges below 6,000 feet. We mapped out a route over the twelve miles of upland muskeg from our landing field to the bottom of the mountain, and, through rifts in the clouds, we caught glimpses of the upper part of the ridge. Suddenly, when we went up the west fork of the Hayes Glacier, the clouds vanished and the peak of Hayes towered eight thousand feet above us, seemingly straight up.

Only then did the Army decide to send an observer from Anchorage—it was a fine time to make up their minds, after we were practically on the glacier! A day later, Lt. Robin Montgomery joined us. Anchorage headquarters seemed especially interested in the way I planned to use air support to approach a big mountain. The service people stationed at Ladd Field in Fairbanks gave us six parachutes for dropping supplies and the Army bombers dropped out the parachute loads for us.

By July 15 we were in camp, and had a working radio that could reach Anchorage, if not yet Fairbanks. Barbara and I went fishing and swimming at a little stream called Ptarmigan Creek, but were devoured by mosquitoes. A day later, we carried seventy-pound packs of gear to Caribou Creek, six miles above our first camp. Our legs were a bit wiggly from staggering through tussocky muskeg. We planned to continue after devouring some hot bouillon, but a huge black cloud whipped down over Hayes and we scarcely had time to put up the tent before we were in a wild tempest of rain and 30 to 50 mph winds.

The wind completely died down during the night, and we had a long, steady grind through dry grass up to the col at the very head of Ptarmigan Creek, overlooking Hayes Glacier. The creek deserved its name: we saw two ptarmigan, and later a female with twelve chicks. That afternoon, a roar announced a bomber in the distance. The plane couldn't possibly have come in worse weather conditions, unless the clouds had been on the ground. But the chutes came down okay. The first one opened only fifty feet above the ground, and its huge load of four forty-pound boxes landed square on the only big rock pile near camp. One box burst open and spilled jam cans all over the ground, but didn't dent even one.

The plane came back five minutes later in a squall of sleet and dropped the second box a quarter of a mile down the hill. We did get word that one of our beer barrels (actually filled with gas) had been pushed out the door by mistake at the end of the glacier about four miles east, but we had planned for double our needs in case something happened to one of the kegs. Other explorers will be amazed to see such a large cask of beer in the wilderness!

By July 20, we had quite a little colony going at the camp we called Bear Ranch Hill, at the base of Hayes. We had three tents up, as well as a cook tent. We saw sixteen Dall sheep on the steep, rocky slopes above our camp at the base of Hayes. They clambered around as we advanced and returned, following every move of ours with their heads erect. It was a superb sight: they looked down on us, silhouetted against the evening sky atop crags at least a thousand feet above.

The next day, we fought gravel, scree, and rotten rock for several demanding hours to reach the 7,000-foot shoulder of Hayes' ridge. There we hit slushy snow six inches deep on black ice. We put on crampons to advance above that, and the ridge looked okay to about 10,000 feet. We got a couple of stunning vistas of the 13,000-foot shoulder of Hayes from our 8,500-foot cache. It was awe-inspiring, but I was more convinced than ever that it was climbable if we got good weather.

My mother, Edith, at Squam Lake, New Hampshire, in the summer of 1950. With the help of live-in nannies and grandparents, we were able to leave our children in safe hands when we were mountain climbing.

It snowed for days, and we rested between intermittent advances to a 9,900-foot camp. A reconnaissance of the pass above required four hours of plowing through fresh snow from knee to waist deep. On July 28, we rose at 7:30 A.M. in a dense fog, after a night of drizzling snow that had added about four inches to the more than two feet of snow from the two days before. Bill Shand, Barbara, and I slept together under two sleeping bags spread out on two air mattresses covered with burlap, and had a pleasant, but crowded night. We had to take terrific loads to clean out camp. I had 103 pounds! The rest, except for Barbara and Henry, carried 80 pounds each.

Mount McKinley was clearly visible between two big peaks at the head of Hayes Glacier, and we watched it from shortly after lunch at 9,600 feet all the way to our next camp at 10,200 feet. We earned a big hot supper of pemmican, chicken, beets, corn, and jam. That night Barbara sewed up a gaping hole on the right side of my pants.

The next day, despite a stiff southwest wind and deep, fresh snow—and against my and Barbara's wishes—the whole party tried to reach the summit. I was against it because of the weather, and because we hadn't yet established camp properly. We hadn't even had a chance to unpack the meat we had brought up from our cache at 9,450 feet.

We started climbing at 8:00 A.M. and struggled for six hours through deep, drifted snow without willow trail markers, pickets, or fixed rope, and finally quit right at the base of the summit cone, at about 13,000 feet. It proved to be a wise decision, because as we reached camp, the whole peak was swept by a violent thunderstorm. We surely would have got caught in it while descending the worst part of the ridge if we had made the summit.

Our next chance, with favorable weather, was August 1. I looked out the tent door at 3:00 A.M., only to be greeted by a wild gust of wind laden with snow. I cuddled back into bed. But an hour later I was awakened by a yell from Sterling saying the weather had changed and we had better start up the mountain.

It was 22 degrees at 6:30 A.M. when we left camp without Henry, who was still fatigued from the earlier attempt. As we climbed, we were frequently in the clouds until we got onto the ridge above the 13,000-foot shoulder. There was a huge banner cloud extending out onto the lee of the peak. The early start gave us enough time to place our fixed ropes and to willow wand the trail so that we would be able to beat a safe retreat to camp.

The pinnacles of the ridge were drifted with fresh, soft snow, but still bore the solid trail I'd kicked and hacked in them before. We swung Barbara into the lead for the last couple of minutes, and at 1:45 P.M., after battling a stiff, cold, westerly breeze and a dozen steep banks of powder snow and drifted, crusty humps, we finally rounded the final dome and stood on the summit of Mount Hayes.

Sterling, Bill, and Ben pulled out a pile of colored confetti from their pockets, which they had stolen aboard ship, and we had a real celebration—it was just like a birthday or wedding party. I made wonderful movies of this. We also couldn't help but wonder what was going to happen to everyone, with the war looming.

We stayed on top for almost an hour. It was icy cold, about 12 degrees, and the wind was sometimes very strong, but we had good sunlight almost the whole time. The distant view was obscured by huge, mountainous clouds, but the overall view was one of the finest I'd ever seen.

We returned to Boston before the end of August, and in late September, Col. L.O. Grice asked me to join a group of cold-weather experts who were going to help the Army do a complete evaluation of all equipment that might be used in arctic or subarctic warfare. It was more than two months before Pearl Harbor, but U.S. involvement in World War II seemed to be inexorably approaching. The group eventually included Sir Hubert Wilkins, Vilhjalamur Stefansson, L. L. Bean, my old friend Bob Bates, and several others with long records of cold weather exploration and survival.

When we climbed Mount Hayes, I thought it likely that years might pass before I got another chance to visit Alaska or climb another mountain. I never would have guessed that service to my country would bring me right back to Alaska in 1942—much less that the U.S. Army was soon going to ask me to climb Mount McKinley.

Chapter Fourteen

Climbing Mount McKinley for the U.S. Army

In 1942 I took a leave from my job as director of the Museum of Science, and for the next three and a half years I was a civilian consultant for the Army on cold-climate equipment. (Neither the Army nor the Air Force wanted to place contracts to buy anything designed by civilians, even if it had been used successfully for years, until it survived formal cold-weather testing.) I served on the U.S. Army Alaskan Test Expedition that made the third ascent of Mount McKinley and lived for nearly three weeks above 15,000 feet; then I was transferred to Washington, D.C., as a full-time expert consultant in the Quartermaster General's office. After that, I was appointed special liaison between the Quartermaster General and Commanding Gen. Simon Bolivar Buckner, Jr., of the Alaska Defense Command, and investigated problems related to the operation of winter equipment on the new Alaska-Canada Highway.

When Colonel Grice came to me in the fall of 1941, he said the Army wanted to use my expertise; they did the same thing with Bob Bates. Bob was unmarried, so they took him into the Army as a captain. I was married with children, and so I didn't actually become a soldier. That turned out to be helpful. I was able to do a lot of things as a civilian that a soldier couldn't do—such as criticize the Army. I could relay observations about what was wrong about stuff. God help you if you tried to criticize the Army when you were part of it.

To be honest, we didn't need to test a damn thing on the trip to Mount McKinley in 1942. We all knew what would work and what wouldn't, but the Army insisted that there be an actual cold-weather test made by the Army itself. Most of the cold-weather experts on our team didn't even go to McKinley. It's true that, as a group, we did improve the ground forces' cold-weather equipment immeasurably, however the cost of the trip was really a waste of money for the government. But they wanted to be able to say that if the equipment worked on Mount McKinley, it would work anywhere. I can understand that.

The U.S. Army Alaskan Test Expedition was conducted under the authority of the Research and Development Branch of the Office of the U.S. Quartermaster General, and the U.S. Air Force research department at Wright Field. It began on May 26, 1942, when I flew out of Minneapolis, and ran until

---

I remember being fascinated by the stories of the early climbs on Mount McKinley. I got to know Belmore Browne quite well; he and Herschel Parker nearly made it to the top way back in 1912. It was a marvelous story: they had climbed to within a few hundred feet of the summit, having started in Seward, and gone by boat and dog team for scores and scores of miles just to get to the bottom of the mountain.

I vividly remember Belmore telling me why they didn't make it. They had just about run out of food, and were living on pemmican. The pemmican had too much fat in it, and they

got sick above 12,000 feet—when they quit, they were only three hundred vertical feet from the top. When I brought pictures back and showed them Belmore, and he said I had exactly the right spot, it made me want to cry to see how close they got. They got down the mountain, the lucky bastards, and suddenly there was a tremendous roar from an earthquake. The whole mountain disappeared for fifteen or twenty minutes in a cloud of wind-driven snow. If Belmore and Parker had completed their climb and stayed on the mountain just a little bit longer, nobody would ever have heard what happened—they would have just disappeared.

As well as being a really competent mountaineer, Belmore was a widely respected artist. In fact, I hired him to paint the black bear exhibit in the lobby of Boston's Museum of Science. In 1954, he had just finished the background, and we went together up to Pinkham Notch in New Hampshire so that we could climb onto what was called Square Ledge. Most years, there's a period after the first snowstorm when there is still autumn color on the trees. Luckily, we were there at that time. He made the picture and put the bear in that scene. He had a hacking cough, and I said, "Belmore, what the hell is wrong with you?" He said, "I simply don't know, but I keep on coughing and coughing."

And that was the last time I saw Belmore Browne alive. Right after that, he went to Yale to start painting a similar background scene and they checked him into the hospital. He had cancer, and died soon after; the black bear mural was his last painting.

nearly the end of August. It was decided to carry out the tests on the upper Harper Glacier at an altitude close to 18,000 feet, between Mount McKinley's twin peaks. That site was midway between major Army and Air Force installations in Anchorage and Fairbanks. That made it easy to parachute, or free-drop, equipment to the field party.

The expedition leader was Lt. Col. Frank Marchman, and the deputy leader was Bob Bates. Peter Gabriel, who had previously climbed with me—now a sergeant—was also on the trip, and Terris Moore, Walter Wood, Sterling Hendricks, and I were listed as consultants.

There were many familiar sights on the way north, including the slopes of Mount Hayes. When we landed at Ladd Field in Fairbanks, we discovered a complicated procedure was in effect. Passwords were exchanged over the radio, followed by predetermined circling, and lowering of the landing gear in a certain spot. The pilot was told to "proceed according to instructions." If he didn't do it right, he had the choice of trying it again, heading back home, or being shot down.

There was plenty of news about a Japanese armada off the Aleutian Islands, and the post was on alert. Everyone had helmets and gas masks available at all times, and armed sentries were everywhere. The commander of base operations viciously opposed our expedition as an "unnecessary ski trip," so we had problems when he attempted to block our flights. Departure plans were also disrupted by Japanese activity in the Aleutians. A steady stream of bombers and pursuit planes headed southwest past us.

I had my thirty-second birthday at Ladd Field, a day after we dropped some supplies near McKinley's McGonagall Pass, but there was less fanfare about that birthday than any I could remember. Barbara telegraphed greetings from Cambridge, Massachusetts, but messages had not been getting through with any regularity. There were constant surprises and delays because of the commander, and it became apparent that if we had been working privately with a commercial airline we would be halfway to McKinley at much less than half the cost.

Mount McKinley had first been climbed in 1913 by Hudson Stuck's party. Nine groups had tried to reach the summit between 1903 and 1913, but no one had tried again for nineteen years until 1932, when a team led by Alfred Lindley and Harry Liek was successful. We were to be next. We approached the mountain from the east side by dog team and on foot to carry supplies that weren't air-dropped, and saw bears, sheep, and wolves on the way, and had wild battles with mosquitoes.

On June 25, while at Wonder Lake cabin, Capt. Jack Bollerud and I experimented with a rubber boat ride across the McKinley River, which was almost impossible to cross on foot. The river was swollen high because of glacier melt from the week's hot weather, and was really roaring. We had a thrilling ride in two big channels, and made the round-trip in an hour. Others were already at an 11,000-foot camp at the head of the Muldrow Glacier.

When I started to move up from Wonder Lake, I felt in grand shape, despite carrying a seventy-five-pound pack for nine miles. The lupine was coming out, fireweed was in full bloom, and yellow daisies and roses were everywhere. By July 2 we were at a heavily supplied camp at 10,400 feet, at the head of the Muldrow Glacier. However, the high temperature was 38 degrees, not the extreme weather the Army was after. Bob Bates appointed me to lead the party that was going to occupy the Upper Basin Camp at 18,000 feet.

On our Fourth of July climb to the end of Karstens Ridge at 14,600 feet, we had magnificent views of Mount Marcus

Baker and what we thought was Mount Sanford. But we also had some unexpected fireworks. One night at about 10:00 p.m., an experimental pressure cooker at full boil with water and instant rice blew up. The cover hit my head—which, luckily, was covered by a fur hat—but the red-hot rice hit the back of Terry Moore's neck, burning him severely. The rice fell between his shirt and back, at 212 degrees, and he just screamed with pain.

We made an emergency trip down for treatment for Terry, covering two horizontal miles and sixteen hundred vertical feet in about fifty minutes. We were both mighty lucky we didn't lose our eyes and get scalded to a crisp. The next day Terry had several bad blisters on his neck, and we named the site Explosion Camp.

At 13,000 feet, our camp was blizzard-bound. What began as snow flurries became a first-class blizzard, blowing up the hillside so hard it rolled us gently to and fro in our sleeping bags. I sincerely hoped we were free of avalanche danger. As we moved higher on the mountain we had trouble maintaining radio contact, and we were running low on supplies by July 8. If we had to retreat for lack of supplies then, the entire venture could be defeated. My impression was that we were in the midst of an utterly disorganized expedition.

At 14,600-foot Browne Tower, the shade temperature was 12 degrees. However, it was like a furnace in the sun. I had nothing on above the waist except for my red flannel underwear. I put a thermometer on my back inside my underwear and obtained a reading of 102 degrees from the direct sunlight!

Einar Nilsson and I climbed the 16,000-foot icefall, topped with an inky layer of black argillite rock, beneath the magnificent pink granite cliffs of McKinley's North Peak. We put on warm clothing—flannel shirts, eiderdown vests, fur hats, and light parkas—and began searching for parachuted supplies from our June 7 air corps dump. A few hundred feet from 18,000-foot Denali Pass, separating the North and South peaks, I noticed a little lump in the snow with a dark end, a hundred yards to our left. It was a "delivery unit." We cut the top open and brought out dried food, cigarettes, bacon, cocoa, macaroni, candy, fifteen pounds of sugar, and five pounds of flour. However, we could not find another box with gasoline that we needed very badly to melt snow into water and cook. Einar and I carried about a third of the contents to our next camp at 18,000 feet, arriving in a thick fog after a long, tough day. Then we retreated to sleep down at 15,000 feet.

The radio was completely useless, but on July 12 we had a beautiful, clear day, with broken clouds below and pretty little

McKinley history met in Fairbanks in the summer of 1949 at the University of Alaska. From left, Bradford Washburn, who led the expedition that pioneered the West Buttress route; Harry Karstens, a member of the first ascent party of 1913 with Hudson Stuck; Charles McGonagall, a member of the 1910 Sourdough Expedition; and Terris Moore, the first to land an airplane above 10,000 feet on McKinley.

cumulus clouds drifting about the two peaks of McKinley. I knew that the nights high on the mountain would linger for a long time in my mind, whether or not we were able to go on to the summit. The air there is full of the ghosts of past climbers: The Fairbanks Sourdoughs of 1910. Belmore Browne. Hudson Stuck. Harry Karstens. Every serac, every steep grade, every rock, and every plateau brought back stories of the pioneers. I hoped we could make the top, if only so that we could enjoy the reminiscences of our trials and tribulations, thirty years later.

Bob Bates came up, and we chatted in the fog about other climbers, the radio, and the war, and he told me that Colonel Marchman's orders were for some, or all of us, to climb to the top of McKinley, if possible, whether or not we were resupplied. The plan was to establish camp near 18,000 feet as swiftly as possible. Clearly, the colonel now felt that climbing McKinley would bring some prestige to the expedition. If the plane never dropped the test equipment we were to stay up high to at least give our clothing, tents, and stoves a thorough test. I estimated that we had about ten days of food, counting a cache that we had discovered from the 1932 climb, the supplies that we had brought up, and the box we had found.

On July 13, we got the radio working and learned that our plane, a DC-3, was scheduled to take off with the equipment, only to be cancelled by the commander, the bastard. The next day two B-24s roared in, but they circled too high above us and dropped the parachutes too fast, destroying some of them, with other boxes drifting far off the mark. Two boxes drifted out of sight a mile to the north and crashed down the abyss at the head of Muldrow Glacier. All in all it was a terribly shameful and sloppy job. Many of the packages were rescued, but others could not be found. Colonel Marchman sent orders for me, Bob, and Sterling to climb the mountain as soon as possible.

We had to get the camp in at the 17,500-foot plateau, but the search for drops that included gasoline went on for days.

On the morning of July 16, Rex Gibson, a Canadian member of our party, suffered an epileptic seizure, and we feared he might die. He had a second fit and was white as a sheet, stiff and frothing at the mouth, his eyes rolled back in his head. Although he stabilized, much effort was given over to trying to move him down the mountain as Einar Nilsson and I moved up.

After three days of snow, Einar and I climbed above Denali Pass and found fourteen boxes and bundles that had been thrown from the planes. Denali Pass and the North Peak were almost cloudless all day, and we had a superb view of Mount Foraker peeking out above a great sea of clouds. The view down into the abyss on the other side of the pass was terrific—a sheer slope of icy, wind-packed snow that would be a formidable job to climb or descend in the conditions of the moment. However, I wrote in my expedition diary, "I'm sure the mountain will be climbed this way some day." (That way was via the West Buttress, and it was a prophetic statement, given that I would lead the first ascent of that route in 1951.)

Einar and I put in a container with supplies and my duffle bag at a campsite that I thought must have been very near to where Stuck's last camp had been. However, the one thing we did not find was gasoline.

By July 19, I had made four trips to 18,000 feet and two to Denali Pass. At that time, no one had ever had the opportunity to become as familiar with McKinley's Great Basin as Einar and I. The next day was gloriously clear, but by evening it was 22 degrees below zero. None of our companions appeared. Einar and I were down to one quart of gasoline. We were not even sure how high we were, though we knew we were above where Stuck had said his "18,500-foot" camp had been. I did not think much of an outfit that would leave members of its party at 18,000 feet, completely out of fuel.

Still, no one came up, and on July 21 Einar and I dropped down to 15,000 feet. When we reached the camp, we found only one member of the party, Peter Webb. After delays, Peter Gabriel and Jack Bollerud had descended to 12,000 feet with Rex Gibson only a day earlier. We participated in a noon radio call, and just as we were inquiring about an emergency gasoline flight, a B-24 swept between McKinley's two peaks. The plane made a drop, but all of the supplies seemed to land at Denali Pass. Einar and I just had to go back up to the pass and search for that gasoline.

The wind was blowing an icy gale, funneling through the pass, when we spotted a parachute. I cut off the shrouds with my ice axe and ripped off the top of the delivery container—it held mail in a small waterproof sack. We had just experienced the highest mail delivery ever in North America. Then, underneath, we saw a five-gallon can of gas.

It was very clear on July 22, and we got word on the radio that Rex Gibson was okay at 10,400 feet. Sterling, Bob, and Peter arrived at the high camp at 5:00 P.M. And at 9:00 P.M., Terry and Jack joined us. It was minus 17 degrees but clear on the morning of the 23rd. Patches of ground fog hung in the hollows, but the sky overhead was really blue. On the radio at 8:00 A.M., Colonel Marchman said, "McKinley will be climbed today!" It was a direct order.

Bob Bates, Terry Moore, Einar Nilsson, and I set off at 11:00 in what felt like hot sun, even though the temperature was just 10 degrees. The whole peak was buried in fresh snow. We took turns leading every two hundred steps, then every hundred steps, and after two hours began changing lead every

Bob Bates and Einar Nilsson on the 1942 U.S. Army cold-weather testing expedition in Alaska.

fifty steps. We reached the first plateau of the northeast ridge at 12:25, and made the altitude at 18,600 feet.

The skies were very disquieting. A cirrus cloud would pop up here and there, then disappear quickly; and a very curious double sun halo appeared. We had a short rest and a bite to eat at 2:15 P.M., at an altitude about the same as the 19,470-foot North Peak. At 3:45 the grade lessened, and we came out on top of Belmore Browne's shoulder. The true top was just a step away up a short, sharp little ridge of real ice, drifted over in spots with fresh snow from the last storm. Bob and Terry went ahead so I could take good pictures of them reaching the top. At 4:10, Einar and I reached their side in the most perfect weather conditions under which McKinley can ever be climbed.

We stayed on top for almost an hour. The descent was easy: powder snow is awful going up, but is often a wonderfully cushioned brake for descending. The next day, Sterling Hendricks, Peter Webb, and Jack Bollerud reached the summit at 1:15 P.M.

However, reaching the summit did not end the assignment—there was still the matter of clearing the mountain, and writing reports. I was the last one left doing expedition work in Fairbanks; then I was ordered to stop in Anchorage to meet with General Buckner and other officers. They seemed concerned, above all, with the consequences of planes going into the water along the Alaska Peninsula and the Aleutian Islands, and what gear might help downed pilots.

On August 18, I was flown on a DC-3 to several locations on the Kenai Peninsula and beyond to the Aleutians, past Mount Redoubt, past Mount Illiamna, to Cape Douglas, Cape Kuliak, and Cape Unalisagvak. We never flew higher than 1,000 feet after leaving Anchorage. We traveled along very savage coastline, big cliffs of vertical rock, past Unalaska Island, and finally to Umnak. I'll never forget a tiny spruce tree that was planted in front of one of the Army buildings there—the only tree on the island, surrounded by a barbed wire fence with a sign reading, "Umnak National Forest—Keep Out!" It was a curious feeling to hear the hum of P-40s and P-38s overhead, and to realize that I was only four hours from the Japanese.

I had a conference with Maj. Jim Starkey about clothing and emergency gear. The fellows in the Aleutians who were fighting wanted emergency gear and plenty of it quick. They needed food packages and emergency kits that could float and be easy to release. I then met with bombardment, pursuit, and Navy pilots. They offered ideas about clothing and emergency equipment.

Two days later I was on a plane again, flying above the Bristol Bay canneries to Naknek and then on to Kodiak. I left Alaska on August 23; by then it was clear that the war was coming closer and closer to home. The battle for the Aleutians was on.

LOVE OF THE HIGH PLACES

The final 2,000 feet of the 12,728-foot Mount Crillon in the Alaska Coast Range. The cliff at the right drops about 7,000 feet to the head of the Johns Hopkins Glacier.

Above: Crillon is in one of the highest coastal mountain ranges in the world. Adams Carter and I made its first ascent on July 19, 1934. Pilot Gene Meyring circled twice around the top to get this image. We were in a Lockheed Vega seaplane. *Right:* An afternoon aerial photo of Mount Crillon's awesome Northwest Face, an 8,500-foot precipice down to the head of North Crillon Glacier.

Left: The terminal ice cliff of South Crillon Glacier at Crillon Lake, Alaska, 1933. *Above:* Bob Bates approaches a huge serac near the 2,000-foot base camp of the National Geographic Yukon Expedition of 1935. We were in the icefall of the Lowell Glacier.

Accompanied by my young wife, we made the first ascent of the 10,182-foot Mount Bertha, in Southeast Alaska, in the summer of 1940.

Left: Barbara joined me in 1941 on the first ascent of the 13,740-foot Mount Hayes, in Alaska's Interior. The 12,000-foot shoulder and the very scary part of the ridge are visible in this aerial photo. Those last thousand feet were just a long, tiring slog up the steep summit slope.

Pages 178 & 179: Sastrugi near Silverthrone Pass, 1945. By the close of World War II, I was part of three more first ascents of Alaska mountains: Mount Deception in 1944, and Mount Silverthrone and nearby Mount Tripyramid in 1945.

Clockwise from left: Barbara looking westward from 18,200-foot Denali Pass, between Mount McKinley's twin peaks, in June 1947. The South Peak is 20,320 feet; the North, 19,470 feet. The time was 5:30 P.M., on July 10, 1951, when I photographed Bill Hackett and Jim Gale, jubilant on McKinley's final windswept summit drift. The world view from McKinley on July 10, 1951, looking southward down the full length of the Kahiltna Glacier. We were reminded of climber Robert Tatum's description of this sight. He was one of four men who made the first ascent of McKinley (on my third birthday, June 7, 1913). He wrote: "The view from the top is like looking out the windows of Heaven." More than a hundred thousand square miles of Alaska is spread out below you.

This is my favorite distant view of Mount McKinley, as seen from Mile 82.1 on the Denali Highway, August 12, 1953, at 8:00 A.M. I took this with infrared film. The tiny spruce trees on the other side of the river are forty feet tall!

Right: The Matterhorn in a summer windstorm, 1958. The air was very rough! *Below:* Back to Chamonix in 1958, where I photographed the Aiguille de la République—a superb granite needle.

Chapter Fifteen

World War II Days in Alaska

One of the Army's great feats on the home front during World War II was building the Alaska–Canada Highway, more than a thousand miles long, and still the main road from the Lower 48 states to Alaska. (Of course, when they built it—in a hurry—it was a dirt road, mostly mud really, but now it is paved.) I visited the Al-Can twice while it was under construction, to study the equipment being used under extreme cold conditions. On my second tour, in 1943, the temperature dropped to minus 63 degrees at one of our road camps, the coldest temperature I've ever experienced.

I was there as a representative of the Quartermaster General's office, to see if the equipment that was supplied actually worked. The entire northern end of the highway was built by the 97th engineers, an outfit of primarily black soldiers from the south. I was always struck by how little sense it made to send those soldiers to the cold of the north at the same time that the Army sent Alaska Scouts, made up of Alaska Natives, to Guadalcanal in the South Pacific. That's why they say there's a right way, a wrong way, and the Army way.

They had four big D-8 tractors with blades in front. The ground was frozen solid, and the first two tractors rolled into the forested wilderness, even pushing forty-foot trees into the bushes. (They never bothered to cut the trees.) Then the second group of tractors would follow behind loaded with gravel, and pour it on top. They were moving as fast as they could, as part of the war effort. In the years since, whenever they've done a construction project or repaving work, they've straightened and smoothed out another section; making it a little bit shorter. But it was an amazing accomplishment.

The original highway was very muddy in the spring, and the rivers overflowed; I remember seeing a bulldozer on a riverbed that was so buried in solid ice that you could only see its exhaust pipe sticking out. That meant six vertical feet of solid ice had to melt before you could use the damned thing. I was inspecting the upper end of the road to find out what was going wrong. They weren't listening to the local experts, the Alaska Road Commission, on how to build a road in that kind of weather. I came upon a group of soldiers in a ditch who were toasting their mittens over the fire to warm them up in minus 30-degree cold!

Another assignment involved the Quartermaster General's desire to minimize the number of pieces of clothing carried by soldiers. They wanted to order, say ten million of one item rather than five million of one and five million of another. Now, the soldiers were issued a jungle sock and a ski sock; both were very comfortable and had wonderful linings. These were the best socks anybody had ever made, but the Quartermaster General wanted to know why we needed two kinds. He wanted to buy one kind. Sir Hubert Wilkins, the pilot, and Stefansson, the explorer, were in this meeting, and Stefansson said, "General, there's only one thing in all of human history that's done two things equally well and that's the human penis." It broke everybody up, and we stayed with two pairs of socks.

The war and the Army changed Alaska quite a bit. When I had made my trips to Alaska, it had been a pretty sleepy place; the war made it a lot busier, active, place. One year during the war I was in Anchorage and walking down the street by myself on Christmas Eve. I heard someone playing a record of Bing Crosby singing "White Christmas," and it made me feel a helluva long way from home. Barbara and the kids were in Massachusetts, and much of the time they didn't even know where I was.

Later in 1943 I was transferred from Washington to Wright Field in Dayton, Ohio, at the personal request of General H. H. Arnold, Commanding General, Army Air Forces, to reorganize the Army Air Forces Flying Clothing and Personal Equipment Program.

Lowell Thomas was a great friend of "Hap" Arnold, and I got to know him very well, too. I was very critical of the quality of the Army's emergency equipment. People at Wright Field wrote the specifications for the equipment, and other people at Patterson Field (also in Dayton) bought the stuff. I had a strong suspicion that the people at Wright Field were in cahoots with suppliers, and that they wrote the specifications so only their friends could be the right bidders. We proved it, and sent a major general to jail for two years.

People just wouldn't believe it when I would say that a lot of Air Force equipment was nowhere as good as it was supposed to be. Part of the problem was that the people who ordered it didn't know a thing about flying, and pilots' real needs.

We would run into first lieutenants who had come back from the combat theater, and they would say that this was lousy, or damn it, that was bad. But people in the Army didn't dare tell a general that the stuff was crappy. In the middle of the war I was frantic about this, and we couldn't get any action, even with my friendship with General Arnold.

Then Dr. Loyal Davis—Nancy Reagan's stepfather, and an expert physician—came back from the fighting in Europe and reported that frostbite exceeded all other casualties of the 8th Air Force Bomber Command combined. Davis had a friend who was President Franklin D. Roosevelt's secretary, and that made it possible to bring a detailed memorandum to the attention of Roosevelt's secretary and of the secretary of war. I did this behind the back of General Arnold, and one morning the lid blew off. I got a telephone call to report to his office immediately. A colonel was in the outer office, and he said, "Brad, go see the general immediately."

General Arnold handed me a letter and told me to read it. I was scared shitless. I thought he was going to see my fine hand behind it all. But the letter said President Roosevelt was supporting change. From then on, better equipment was developed.

Being involved with cold-weather equipment, and being considered a specialist on the subject, meant that often enough I was assigned to Alaska for various tasks. Before the war ended, I was part of three more first ascents of Alaska mountains: Mount Deception in 1944, and Mount Silverthrone and nearby Mount Tripyramid in 1945.

CHAPTER SIXTEEN

INVESTIGATING A
TRAGIC ACCIDENT

I was in Fairbanks in late fall 1944, and we learned that a C-47 Air Transport Command plane flying from Anchorage to Fairbanks had just disappeared. People were searching and searching and couldn't find it anywhere. Then, one of the searchers flying through a pass saw a bright light in the general area where they had been looking. It was late afternoon, and the sun was hitting a window and reflecting up from the wreckage of the plane, at least twenty miles away. It was like a signal.

The plane had been carrying a bunch of GIs on their way home on leave to see families. The commanding general in Anchorage called me in from Ladd Field and asked what could be done about this. I said that everyone had to have been killed in the crash and to reach the crash site would involve considerable danger to the search party. Since the passengers were certainly all dead, why go?

The reply was that I was not being asked how I could get to the wreckage, I was being ordered to go there, danger or no. It turned out that a Congressman's son was among the victims, and there was big pressure on the general to find out what caused the crash.

This was mid-October. By the time we were able to fly in

At 10,100 feet on November 11, 1944. I was among those investigating the site of a C-47 plane crash on Mount Deception.

and reach the plane, it was already half-buried in snow. It had clearly hit the top of a nearby mountain, one which was unmapped and didn't have a name at that time. There was a west wind, and the pilot apparently had dropped his left wing. You could see that it had scoured along the hillside first, and then the left-hand engine had smashed into the hillside. After that, the airplane went end-over-end, sixteen hundred feet down a shelf that couldn't be climbed from below. The engine was still stuck in the hillside. I looked over the scene and said, "The only way you can get to this site is to go up the mountain from the north side and then go down to the wreckage."

This peak is now called Mount Deception; and it is 11,826 feet high. The actual route would take the investigating party over a pass a couple of hundred yards below the summit. Grant Pearson, the chief Denali National Park ranger, was asked to join, along with Jim Gale, a top sergeant in the Air Force. (Jim later became a close friend, and climbed Mount McKinley with me twice.)

Grant, who was in charge of the field party, was insistent that the plane had run into Mount Brooks, another tall peak in that area. I said, "Hell, it didn't run into Mount Brooks at all." You couldn't argue with Grant, so we had to go up there. We went up the Brooks Glacier and nearly to the top of Mount Deception, and there was the wreckage way below us on the other side. We had to climb an extremely steep snow slope from Brooks Glacier, and then come down the other side of Deception to reach the plane.

We finally got down the hill to the wreckage. It was very difficult; we had to put a fifty-foot fixed rope in a short, almost vertical bit of the hillside just to reach it. We dug and dug, and got everything out of the plane—except for bodies. Not a single body was down there in the snow. The plane was filled with playing cards, thrown all over the debris, and the seat belts in the cabin were all undone. Everyone must have been moving around and playing cards, when the plane hit and burst into two parts. I think the force threw them all out one end of the plane. Due to specific gravity, human bodies in a snowslide will go down to the bottom of the avalanche. The airplane, being so big, probably floated on the crest of the slide.

We did find the copilot's suitcase, with his name on it, which I will never forget: Lt. J. J. Bliven. We opened it up, and there were his neatly folded underwear, socks, and pajamas, and a bottle of Scotch whiskey. He had been on his way to someplace that was home. The investigating party drank the whiskey in no time.

The only good thing that came out of that trip was meeting Jim Gale. Jim and I were asked if we were willing to take close-up pictures of the plane's engine. I realized that the only way to reach it was to climb up over the pass near the top of Mount Deception and rope down to it. (He and I called it Mount Deception just because we liked the sound of it.)

We made our way down to the engine, embedded in the hillside; using pliers and a chisel, we removed the markings so we could prove that it was the engine from the crashed plane. We had a hell of a time getting back up to the ridge, and had to be pulled through a cornice like sacks of meal after we took our last pictures. Snow went down our necks and in our shirts as we were dragged up onto the ridge, where we were greeted by a frigid northwest wind that had come up during the hour we were below.

When the work was done, a handful of us said, "Let's go to the summit and make the first ascent of the mountain." We cut loose the ropes, tightened up our parkas, and climbed quickly to the top of Mount Deception; exactly one thousand feet above our camp. It was November 14, 1944.

The next April, I was sent back to Interior Alaska and climbed Mount Silverthrone (13,220 feet) and Mount Tripyramid (11,720 feet). Once again the assignment was cold-weather gear testing. Silverthrone is just east of Mount McKinley. Bob Sharp, who had been with me on Mount Deception, and Frank Foster, a doctor, were with me.

We were testing the new tents and clothing that had come out of all of our earlier tests. They had us in two groups of two, one who knew how to use all of the equipment and could monitor the situation, and the other who knew nothing about it. Frank would act as a plain soldier seeing the equipment for the first time.

We walked into the Muldrow Glacier from the Denali Highway, and created a scenario. They were inexperienced passengers in an airplane who had to use the emergency kit and equipment. I instructed them that if they were short on water they could always make water from ice, not snow. (Ice makes water 1-to-1; snow makes water 10-to-1.)

The next day we had to cross a stream and I fell through the ice. I went in clear to my waist and it was about minus 25 degrees. Now we had a real emergency. We rushed up the valley to a place where we could put up a tent, and I went back down to get my pack, which I had thrown to the other side of the creek. I told them, "You guys must make some hot water as fast as you can, because when I get back I will need to have some hot, hot tea."

What do you suppose they were doing when I got back? They were melting snow, after I had just told them that ice was better; besides, they were right next to a flowing stream. I said, "For Christ's sake, all you have to do is go out the back door to get water." They were busy following regulations.

Mount Silverthrone was not a hard climb at all, and neither was Tripyramid, which is next to it. The view from the top of

Silverthrone is the best view you can get of McKinley, anywhere. Silverthrone is 13,000 feet high, the valley between it and McKinley is 5,000 feet, and McKinley is 20,000. It's a magnificent view, but I imagine very, very few people go in there.

We completed the first ascent of Silverthrone on April 12, 1945, and the first ascent of Tripyramid on April 17. It was a matter of being in the area and taking advantage of the opportunity. We put plenty of cold-weather equipment to good use, and gave it a helluva test.

At the end of World War II, I received the Exceptional Service Award; a special letter of commendation from H. H. Arnold, Commanding General of the Army Air Forces; and another from Robert A. Lovett, assistant secretary of war. After three and a half years of cold-weather work, I returned to my family and resumed my job as director of the museum that, in December 1945, became Boston's Museum of Science.

Barbara and I were on McKinley again in 1947 for "Operation White Tower," an expedition with multiple sponsors, among them the museum and RKO Radio Pictures. Here Barbara prepares a huge load in Anchorage for later free-fall drop to our 18,000-foot camp at Denali Pass.

Chapter Seventeen

BACK TO McKINLEY — WITH BARBARA

In November of 1946, not too long after I was settled back into my life at the museum, I got a phone call from Paul Hollister in New York, with RKO Radio Pictures, saying he wanted to have lunch with me "as soon as possible" in Boston to discuss an exciting idea they had. Hollister wanted me to lead an expedition to climb Mount Everest. They had gotten the idea from *The White Tower*, a novel by James Ramsey Ullman, who wrote many books about mountaineering. They had purchased the rights to the book, and wanted to give favorable publicity to mountaineering. They wanted to increase attention to help make the movie a hit when it came out, and to test camera equipment at high altitude in the cold, in anticipation of making the movie.

Even though I would have loved to go to Mount Everest, I knew it was just not possible. After World War II, China and Nepal were closed to foreigners. You couldn't get into those countries to climb the mountains. I suggested we take an expedition up Mount McKinley instead. I was familiar with McKinley, and I knew we could also do cosmic ray studies in Denali Pass. (At the time, the Naval Research office was very interested in cosmic radiation, and I knew that if the museum

Collecting rock samples just above Denali Pass, early June 1947.

was going to let me go for several months, there had to be real scientific work to be done.)

The Office of Naval Research had a guy at the University of Chicago named Hugo Victoreen, an expert in the field, who wanted to go with us and get as high as he possibly could for cosmic ray study. (The higher you got, the more powerful were the cosmic rays that got through the atmosphere.) I said, "Sure, we'll take readings for you, but you've got to pay for the trip." RKO also gave us $25,000. Then, when they found out that Barbara might want to go on the climb, they got excited. International News and RKO Radio Pictures said, "This is marvelous. This will give us more publicity, to have along the first woman who has ever climbed McKinley."

So, in the spring of 1947, Barbara and I were off to Alaska again. The expedition was named "Operation White Tower," and it was sponsored by the museum and RKO Radio Pictures, with help from Northwest Airlines, the University of Chicago's physics department, the U.S. Geodetic Survey, the Office of Naval Research, and the National Park Service.

We put together a very impressive team of thirteen people, including Grant Pearson, Jim Gale, Capt. Bill Hackett of the Army, and George Browne, the son of Belmore Browne. George, a painter like his father, hoped to complete the climb his father came so close to making thirty-five years earlier.

After months of intense organizing, Barbara and I left Boston on the evening of March 23. We tucked the children into bed, watched them fall sound asleep, and left for Alaska. We had a live-in nanny at the time, and grandparents lived close by. On the way north, Barbara and I met the press in New York and Minneapolis. The International News Service had made a deal for exclusive rights to the story—which caused some friction, as I was talking to the press freely. We landed in Anchorage at midday on March 28, just in time for a snow squall.

Thousands of pounds of supplies were already moving to the Muldrow Glacier. McKinley towered above the Susitna Lowlands and was the coldest looking sight I'd ever seen, with a wee, frigid banner cloud floating just in the lee of the peak. On the 30th, George Browne accompanied me on a flight. The Susitna River, the Ruth Glacier, and Anderson Pass were old landmarks for his father, and George was thrilled to see each spot where his dad had had his great experiences. Despite the cold, George did some excellent paintings of McKinley while we were on the mountain. (They were out of public view for many years, after his untimely death in an accidental shooting, only to reemerge on display at the Anchorage Museum of Art and History a few years ago.)

When we got out of the plane at 5,700 feet, it was warm and calm. I walked over to the edge of the glacier with the boys, and located the old 1942 campsite, pointing out exactly where to put our tents. We set them up on dry ground instead of snow and ice. Barbara and I joined the camp for the duration on April 9. One thing that had changed from my early climbs in Alaska was the quality of the food. Frozen food is a treat—and we got lots given to us for free. We ate strawberries our first night on the glacier, and the next night had delectable green beans and chicken a la king, with fresh peaches for dessert.

We had a bit of a scare on the 13th. Grant Pearson, Jim Gale, and Bob Craig set off to reconnoiter the upper glacier. Grant was leading, with Jim in the middle of the rope only a few feet off the trail, which they had been marking with willow wands. Bob inched up beside Grant, but just before they reached really solid ice, without the slightest warning, Bob fell into a hidden crevasse and disappeared instantly. Jim fell on his ice axe on the bare ice, fifty feet behind them, and Grant managed to fall backward just before he would have stepped into the hole, too.

Jim lost his ice axe and started slipping slowly but steadily towards the crevasse, and Bob, who had had his vertical fall stopped about ten feet down, kept sliding in deeper—dangling in the air in a sixty-foot hole. Grant managed to hustle over to Jim and stop his slide about six feet from the edge of the crevasse. They pulled Bob up to an ice block wedged in the crack, then lowered his crampons. Then they pulled and he climbed.

Earl Norris and his dog team carry a load of freight up Mount McKinley's Muldrow Glacier, just above McGonagall Pass, 1947.

It was glare ice all around the crack, and he was in the hole for ninety minutes. Those fellows learned a serious lesson: don't walk with a loose rope anywhere on a glacier.

Our dog driver was Alaskan Earl Norris, who became famous soon after for winning the Anchorage Fur Rendezvous World Championship sprint race, and for decades afterward was known for his expertise in breeding Siberian huskies. He arrived with the dogs two days later, but did not have an easy mush. It was a miserable trip—the whole sled went through the thin ice of Clearwater Creek, and the lowlands were rotten going. But the next day, Earl and others moved up to establish Camp I below the Muldrow Glacier icefall at 7,500 feet. The dogs took a five-hundred-pound load four miles up-glacier, and had hellish going with a foot of loose, new snow.

We started up McKinley at last on April 26 in dense fog, but we had a glorious sunset, with pink seas of clouds over the lowlands to the northeast. Barbara and I settled into a 7 x 7 Logan tent with lining. We had a big firepot for a stove, but no light except for a flashlight. She had to shake out her frozen socks and insoles in the tent. It was about 50 degrees on the floor, but more than 100 degrees six feet above in the peak of the tent! The next day was our seventh wedding anniversary.

A day later our pilot, Hakon Christenson, arrived in a small Waco airplane on skis and made good time, bringing Bill Sterling, an *Anchorage Times* reporter. But when he tried to take off, he couldn't get going. He had a thin, tacky slush on the soft powder, which was nearly a foot deep, and a 5 mph crosswind from the south. He took five tries and gave up, deciding to wait till the snow froze. He brought in lettuce, onions, mayonnaise, cucumbers, tomatoes, and carrots as a surprise and that night we had a real salad. The delay was only brief; after repeated tries, they finally managed to take off.

Shorty Lange turned twenty-two the day we got two relays up the hill behind camp, and Earl took a load to Camp II at the Great Icefall at 8,500 feet. We gave Shorty a birthday candle at supper on a tin plate covered with snow, and then had frozen strawberries for dessert. The floor of the tent caved in because of the heat of the stove; then, after we'd made adjustments, the glacier moved with a big jerk and a loud grunt. The tent was pitched right on a crevasse. It was the first time Barbara and Bill Sterling had ever felt a glacier move.

Day after day we took movies and hauled supplies. The

clouds came and went, occasionally leaving more snow; it was minus 12 on May 3. This trip was the first time I had used igloos in place of tents; Jim Gale was an expert at building them. (One day we got hit by a blizzard at 16,000 feet—Jim built an igloo on the spot, and we holed up for a couple of days until the storm blew itself out.)

All you need to build an igloo is a saw and maybe a knife to cut the blocks, assuming you've got hard snow. Good igloo snow is wind-packed so hard you can walk on it without sinking. An igloo has an amazing number of attributes that a tent doesn't have. It doesn't flap in the wind, so even in a helluva storm, it is totally silent. In a tent, you never get any sleep in a big wind, and you have to get up in the middle of the night to fix the guy ropes because they are thrashing around. (I'll never forget going out in big storms to relieve myself. People would say, "How do you do that at minus 20 degrees at 18,000 feet?" And I would reply, "It's very simple. Faster than you've ever done it before.")

Another good thing about an igloo is that you didn't have to carry it from camp to camp. Finally, the inside of an igloo never gets really cold. It can be minus 20 outside, and the temperature inside will be around 25 degrees above. Just the presence of people breathing inside makes a difference, and if you have a stove, it can get really hot. You can make an igloo impermeable by turning the stove up to 90 degrees, then patting the inside with your hand, creating an internal layer of igloo ice. We used igloos several times on McKinley in 1951.

Looking southward up Brooks Glacier from Muldrow Glacier. In December, sunrise and sunset occur at almost exactly the same time!

Camp III was established at 11,000 feet on May 7. It was minus 3 overnight, still chilly. As I took pictures, George painted like a fury. And then, as we cleared the cache below for a climb back up to 11,000, movies were shot. At the end of the day we had an airdrop of supplies from a C-47 airplane. For the first time we were able to direct the airdrop passes by radio, and that improved their accuracy. Jim lit a red smoke flare to show the area. He yelled, "Now!" to me, waiting in the tent door, and I in turn hollered, "Drop, drop, drop!" into the radio. I was always a bit leery about being hit, and kept my head out the door after each yell. Everything landed within a 150-yard radius of camp.

When the attack on the summit began in earnest we found our 1942 fixed rope still there at 13,200 feet. I was astonished. After a fifteen-minute search we found thermometers from 1942 at 14,500 feet. I opened the wooden case breathlessly, only to find to my disgust that the box had lost one end, and was full of icy snow. One thermometer read 60 degrees and the other read minus 40; the actual temperature that day was minus 8.

On May 15, Barbara and I camped together—and alone, a rare situation for us—in an igloo at 12,000 feet on Karstens Ridge, after a beautiful afternoon climb from 11,000 feet. The valley and peaks to the east were covered with clouds and Karstens Ridge and 14,600-foot Browne Tower and McKinley's North Peak were all clear. The next day was the first time Barbara and I had ever been entirely alone on a rope, and it was a thrill to climb Karstens Ridge together. We did the whole trip from 12,000 to 14,600 feet in three and three-quarter hours, with a stop for a thermos of hot coffee, crackers, and chocolate at the 13,500-foot cache.

On the 20th, Jim and I were caught in a wild southwest storm on the edge of the 16,500-foot plateau in a 7 x 7 tent at the cache we had put in. The wind and blowing snow were too furious to continue. After it cleared, we heard on the radio that a group of three University of Alaska students—Gordon Heereid, Morton Wood, and George Schuman—were starting their own climb of McKinley, beginning by driving the road to Camp Eielson.

The wind started howling and snow fell again as Jim and I fought our way to Denali Pass. At least a hundred times we had to turn our backs to that downvalley wind, and brace ourselves until a gust had blown itself out. Barbara ended up alone at the 14,600-foot camp for a day. What a rotten shame that the bad weather kept us separated for so long.

Barbara and I stood on the 20,320-foot summit of Mount McKinley on June 6, 1947 (at twenty below zero with a brisk breeze!).

We were spread out all over the mountain on the 23rd, each group reporting a storm where it was located. Jim and I hunkered down in an igloo at 16,500 feet for two days. There was a terrific gale pinning us down, and we were running out of gasoline. Our fuel conservation program meant staying in the sleeping bag almost all day. McKinley surely was putting up a fight. We needed patience to outlast the weather. (Some key components of the cosmic ray apparatus were also blown away in the huge storm.) I was stuck inside so long I became convinced that my rear end had done more work than any other part of my body on the expedition.

A B-17 made a resupply run on May 29, and the radio report called the conditions "the most turbulent we've ever flown in." The airdrop worked, however, and we had a new batch of gasoline, tins of beef and gravy, chocolate bars, canned hams, and coffee. More airdrops followed over the next few days, and we finally reassembled much of the team at 18,000 feet.

The weather was flawless on June 6 as Barbara, Grant, George, and RKO photographer Bill Deeke left camp at 10:30 A.M., headed for McKinley's summit. Shorty and I did some survey work, and then followed with Jim and Bob Craig, each carrying forty pounds of camera and survey gear. At about 19,000 feet, Grant said he was having trouble with his heart, and retreated to camp. The rest of us plodded along with wonderful views in all directions.

At 1:00 P.M. the weather began to look decidedly unsettled. A cloud cap covered nearby Mount Foraker and a high southerly overcast began to appear below us. It was obvious that we must race, or we wouldn't make it to the top of the South Peak, the true summit at 20,320 feet. I pushed ahead as fast as possible, unroped, up the summit cone, closely followed by Shorty and Bill Hackett. Barbara untied from the others and, to my happy amazement, forged on ahead of them to join us for lunch halfway up that last, steep summit slope.

We had a dandy warm lunch at minus 10 in the sun without any wind, but it was cold enough to keep us standing. After lunch, we roped up: Bob Craig, Shorty, Bill, Barbara, and I together. The snow was hard at first, but got quite deep in the lee of the summit shoulder. After climbing a short little ice cliff in forty minutes, we came out onto the shoulder about two hundred feet below the top.

The weather to the south looked evil. I unroped and let Barbara and the boys go ahead, up to the magnificent, frost-feathered cornices of the last two hundred yards. I photographed them until my hands were numb in the 15–25 mph breeze (at nearly minus 20). Bill Deeke, George, and Jim arrived fifteen minutes later. I hustled after Barbara's rope,

Surveying atop Mount McKinley, June 1947.

and reached the top fifteen minutes after her at 4:15 P.M. They had the American flag up. We were still in bright sunshine, but a storm was gathering.

Barbara was in top form and was helping me take pictures. Later, she said her impression of the view from the summit of McKinley was exactly as Robert Tatum, with Hudson Stuck during the first ascent in 1913, had said—it was like looking out the windows of heaven.

There was an icy wind as we planted an eight-foot bamboo pole just north of the tip-top survey marker. My hands were never colder, and my fingers were numb handling my theodolite. We all shook hands, and it was about 5:30 when we started down. It was a dramatic moment for me, one of sadness, happiness, and triumph all mixed together. It was my second time at the summit, and I thought it would be the last time in my life. I was already the only person to have climbed to the top twice, and now Barbara was the first woman to reach the summit. I was very proud of her accomplishment. Even though others had wondered before the climb, I was confident she could do it. She never seemed to get very tired, and she fit in with the group with ease.

The descent was easy once the wind died: it only took us an hour to reach high camp.

The next day—my thirty-seventh birthday—dawned beautifully, and by late morning we were on the trail again with the theodolite, headed to the lower, 19,470-foot North Peak, which almost no one climbs these days. We climbed to the top of an eight-hundred-foot steep pitch above camp in a little over an hour without any wind, then dropped gently across the half-mile-wide plateau between that cliff and the North Peak's final cone. We surveyed on top of the North Peak for nearly three hours before returning to camp. It was unbelievably pleasant; we didn't even need gloves. Between observations, I laid my notebook in the snow and the pages didn't rustle a bit. We accomplished a pretty good double-header in two days, and Barbara became the first woman to climb both peaks of Mount McKinley—another great achievement for her. Again, I was very proud.

We got the word of our success out by radio, and soon received congratulations by telegram from the National Geographic, from family members, the Science Museum, Terry Moore, and the International News Service.

On June 11, Barbara and I descended ahead of the others, and at about 12,500 feet ran into the three students we had been told were trying to climb the mountain on a shoestring. As I reached them, I said, "Dr. Livingstone, I presume." But they didn't get it.

We completed our survey, made our movie, climbed the mountain, put the first woman on the summit, and provided good publicity for RKO and mountaineering. Although the views from the Denali Pass confirmed my feeling that McKinley probably could be climbed more easily from the West Buttress than up the seemingly endless Muldrow Glacier— especially if an airplane was used for the approach—I did not believe I would ever be back on the mountain again.

A year or two after it was all finished, the Office of Naval Research wrote me a letter saying that no additional cosmic ray studies would be needed, because the atom-smashing equipment they were using at sea level was producing higher velocity particles than the cosmic rays. That had been the big reason for the government to support us, and it turned out that what we did was ultimately irrelevant. But we got a helluva good trip out of it.

CHAPTER EIGHTEEN

A CRAZY MISADVENTURE
IN CHINA

For about twenty-five years, it had been rumored that a mountain called Amne Machin in Northwest China might be taller than Mount Everest's then-listed height of 29,000 feet. In January 1948, I signed on as scientific director of an expedition that was going to try to find out if it was true. The three months I spent in China accounted for what might be the strangest episode of my career.

People talked about this high mountain, but no one had ever seen it. They were saying it was 30,000 feet high. This was right after World War II, and just before the Chinese Communist revolution. *Life* magazine asked me if I would be willing to go out into the field and investigate. I said, sure, I would love to investigate, but it was going to be very expensive, and I needed someone to pay the bill. The Museum of Science agreed to be a cosponsor and let me go, provided that my salary was paid by the financial backer.

Appearing on the scene was Milton Reynolds, the ballpoint pen king from Chicago, who, with his pilot Bill Odom, had recently made the fastest flight around the world. He had made a fortune on the patent for the first ballpoint pens (and somebody said he had also made a fortune selling secondhand tires). We met to discuss things, and he agreed to finance the trip. He was eager for publicity, and the agreement was that I would be scientific director, but he would be the overall leader. Because he was known to be an unpredictable fellow, the contracts were drawn up in great detail. Part of the agreement allowed me to choose a competent scientist whom Reynolds would pay adequately.

On visits to Washington, Reynolds stated he had secured permission from the Chinese government for the expedition. It later turned out that the Chinese government had not given its permission, and had only "expressed its welcome." It rapidly appeared that Reynolds was more interested in the publicity than anything else. I was not at all happy about it, nor was Bill Gray, who was the Far Eastern head of *Life*.

I was designated to make an advance trip to China to complete the negotiations and, at the last minute, Reynolds joined me. We made a deal that although Odom would be our pilot, the Chinese would have a copilot, their own scientists, and a defense office representative along on the flights. Bill Odom got things off to a bad start by saying, "I won't have any goddamned chink in the cockpit beside me."

We started in Shanghai, but as the weather warmed up, we faced a large number of storms. It was decided that we were better off trying to leave from Peking, way north of Shanghai, so we went there. Bill Odom seemed to think that he was the best pilot who ever lived. We had a war surplus C-87 plane that Reynolds called "Explorer." However, its capability and equipment were misrepresented to us, and several times Odom refused to fly because of "inclement" weather even when Chinese commercial airplanes were flying.

While we were trying to get the expedition moving, Reynolds and I were invited to have tea with Mrs. Chiang

Kai-shek. Madame Chiang was wearing overshoes because there was a little bit of snow on the ground, and I recall that the ends of her shoelaces were mink tails.

She invited us to visit her farm to see her cows. I've never seen more cows; in the middle of this endless herd was a pen about eight feet square, built of plywood, full of sawdust, and there was a mother cow with a little baby next to it. Madame Chiang said, "I wish you could have been here yesterday when I was present when this baby was born." Just then the cow blew a huge fart, telling us that Madame Chiang had had nothing whatever to do with this birth.

In Peking, there were revetments—forty-foot square walls of dirt where you could park planes, which would be protected from nearby explosions. Bill Odom was warned in advance to be very careful, because it was spring and the ground surface was muddy. He was told that if he got his wheels outside of the revetment's brick surfaces, he might get into real trouble. Odom, always eager for a chance to show off his ability, spun our airplane 90 degrees to enter the revetment, and his left wheel went into the mud so deep that the left wing was only about three feet above the mud.

There we were in Peking with the airplane stuck in the mud. I was with a very nice guy from MIT named Walt McKay, and we decided we wanted no more of this show. We decided Odom was crazy, and what they were trying to do was completely disorganized. We wanted to get the hell out. Somebody had a friend called "Newsreel" Wong, and he agreed to lend us the money to fly back to Shanghai.

The Chinese had a neat plan to get the plane out of the mud. Instead of trying to jack it up, they dug down on the right side, so that the plane was level, and then they made a ramp. Odom gave the plane full power and it came right out.

The Chinese were furious at Odom and Reynolds because they were ignoring the observers, who we had agreed to have along with us at every step. They were ordered to Nanking to explain themselves.

At that point, Reynolds, who had disparaged the scientific objectives of the trip, officially called off the expedition. Then, as McKay was getting ready to leave the country, Reynolds made several pronouncements that "no one was to blame" for what had happened, and that "all of us must equally share responsibility for this." Then he warned McKay directly, saying, "If necessary, to protect my interests, I will make things up and the public and press will believe Bill Odom and me, and not you." Actually, we felt a great sense of relief that the farce had ended with no personal injury. Every single member of the party had lost any vestige of faith in the leader of the expedition and his pilot.

Reynolds and Odom were pretty clever guys. They had been telling the Chinese that they had to keep the gas tanks full, because it was so hot that the gas could mix with condensation and explode. The next thing we knew, Reynolds and Odom had disappeared with their crew chief. Word got around that they were going to fly over Everest and Amne Machin and then land in Calcutta.

So they left the rest of us without fares home, without saying good-bye to the Chinese scientists, and without paying the hotel bill. And then we were amazed to learn that Reynolds and Odom were back on the ground in Shanghai because they didn't have permission to land in India. All hell broke loose. Everybody was mad at everybody. According to the press, they were in Shanghai with the plane's gas tanks full, with everybody arguing and furious at them; then at dawn, Reynolds, complete with airplane, disappeared again.

Dr. Sah Pen-Tung of China had accused Reynolds of trying to freeze out the Chinese and American scientists; because of his complaint, the plane had been surrounded by armed guards. But the plane was gassed up. Reynolds and Odom told the guards that the motors had to be run occasionally to stay sharp and make sure everything was okay. And then they began to move the plane. The guards ran over with their rifles, and Reynolds, who had boasted about his $35 "gold" pens (which actually had cost about 50 cents each), began throwing handfuls of these pens out the window.

The guards rushed to pick up the pens that they thought were gold, and the airplane took off for America. Jack Cabot—one of the Boston Cabots—was the U.S. consul in Shanghai, and he was fuming. He said, "This is outrageous. I'm gonna stop this son of a bitch." Reynolds had to stop in Hawaii to refuel, and Cabot got word to Gen. Douglas MacArthur, who was in charge there, to stop him and hold him. But MacArthur wanted to run for president, and Reynolds was wealthy and influential, so he just let him go on home to Chicago.

By then, Reynolds and Odom had stopped in Japan and told their version of the story to the Associated Press. The story that went out on the wire service, with a dateline of Tokyo, began:

> *Milton Reynolds arrived here late last night on an unauthorized flight from Shanghai, saying he made a melodramatic getaway by flinging ball-point pens at gun-brandishing Chinese guards.*
>
> *The Chicago millionaire declared he fled to escape a financial shakedown and that his ill-fated quest for the world's highest mountain had already cost him $250,000.*
>
> *Reynolds reported he got into his impounded exploration plane with his crew of three by promising the Chinese some of the pens which made him a fortune.*

"They eagerly followed me; I got in and threw out the pens—50 of them—and slammed the door," he said.

Then pilot Bill Odom gunned the engines. As tommy-gun-toting guards came running, he turned on one wheel and roared off the runway downwind. Guards scattered like frightened chickens.

"I saw one guard with a tommy gun who was so surprised his jaw was falling off," remarked Odom. "I guess he forgot to shoot."

The whole thing was a ghastly fiasco, and after three months in China working on this, I just wanted to go home. Bill Gray of *Life* sent word back to Peking that Washburn and McKay will tell all unless they are given first-class air fare from Shanghai to New York. Our tickets were received almost instantly.

I never believed that there was a mountain higher than Everest. Eventually, Amne Machin was explored; my good friend Terris Moore later made the first ascent of the mountain. It turned out to be around 24,000 feet high (and, incidentally, a much more difficult climb than Everest). It was quite magnificent to look at, and if you were a pilot traveling in cloudy weather, it must have looked enormous.

Not too much later, Bill Odom entered a national flying competition in which you had to fly around pylons; he had never done anything like that in a small plane. Apparently, he cut a turn too tight, blacked out, and crashed. The plane exploded and burned, and Bill Odom was killed.

CHAPTER NINETEEN

BUILDING BOSTON'S
MUSEUM OF SCIENCE

The period immediately after the trip to China was one of the most crucial and rewarding in my career as director of Boston's Museum of Science. On December 14, 1949—eighty-seven years after the Commonwealth of Massachusetts had given us the land for the old museum on Berkeley Street—we laid the cornerstone for the first building at Science Park. This was the East Wing, and it cost almost $1 million—fund-raising had been going on for years, and thousands of people around New England had made contributions. This was only going to be about one-quarter of our ultimate physical plant. We had dreams and plans for a planetarium, a Hall of Nature, a Hall of Man and Public Health, a Hall of Science and Industry, and two auditoriums.

In my remarks for the occasion, I pointed out that the building lay precisely on the boundary between Boston and Cambridge. However, I added, "We intend it to be a vital, active science center for all of New England."

I quoted the words of President Amos Binney in his annual report of 1845, thinking ahead to what the old museum could become. "We would, in short, establish a museum as the present condition of science calls for, such a one as the high character of

The Museum of Science "First Team" in the iron shelter that later became our temporary office, September 11, 1949. From left is Mary Morgan, Lorraine Welsh, Mary Desmond, Kay Callahan, me, Clyde Albee, Archie Paris, and Val Wilcox. The only missing person was John Patterson.

our community would lead strangers to expect to find here, and such a one as we, citizens of no mean city, should be proud of."

"Today, as in 1845, this is our objective," I said. "A live, active, modern institution—one of which every New Englander can truly be proud."

An impressive collection of symbolic items was interred in the cornerstone:

• Each of the six New England governors sent local soil that, as part of the ceremony, was combined in one container to symbolize the museum's dedication for service to all New England.

• Ludlow Griscom, president of the Boston Society of Natural History, presented a packet containing plans for the museum, a history of the society since its founding in 1830, and a file of letters from the honorary sponsors.

• J. Willard Hayden, president of the Charles Hayden Foundation, presented an illustrated report of the accomplishments of the museum's most active extension program, the Hayden Camp Tours, which annually brought ten thousand children to summer camps to learn about nature.

• Norman D. Harris, the museum's director of education, presented a vial containing several hundred million living cells, in a state that we believed to be the closest to suspended animation then achievable. The vial was prepared by Dr. William H. Weston of Harvard, who had instantly frozen the contents at a very low temperature, then dehydrated and sealed them in a tiny tube, in a vacuum. We expected some of the cells to live for as much as a hundred years.

• The Polaroid Corporation of Cambridge took photographs of the ceremony with cameras that developed pictures in less than a minute, and Dr. Edwin H. Land presented the pictures to all those present. For the first time in history, photographs of a ceremony like this could be placed in the cornerstone on the spot.

Then the governor of Massachusetts, Paul A. Dever, sealed all of the materials into a copper cornerstone container. It was a great occasion.

Carl Compton, head of MIT, was one of those present. After Carl died some years later, I went to a huge convocation in his honor in the Great Court of MIT. The head of Trinity Church said that Carl had always kept on his desk a quotation from Aristotle: "The search for truth is in one way hard and in another way easy, for it is evident that no one can master it fully or miss it wholly. But each adds a little to our knowledge of nature, and from all the facts assembled there arises a certain grandeur." This statement applied to the museum as we wished to expand it. As each three or four years went by, the museum became a little more important, which made it easier to raise money for the growing thing.

Through the years, more and more schools sent young children to the museum, but I was not solely interested in educating children. We were focused on the education of the general public. Many of the kids brought their families back into the museum on weekends, after the kids had been brought there by their schools. The kids loved it, and more importantly, learned that learning is exciting. We brought learning to them in three dimensions.

When we prepared to build our second building, the Hayden Planetarium, I got a nasty phone call from the guy who ran the American Museum of Natural History in New York, where the first Hayden Planetarium was located. He said we were not to use the name Hayden because it would confuse people. The New York planetarium had been built with money from Charles Hayden, and I was friends with his brother Willard. I went to see Willard. He had a pretty good sense of humor, and said, "You tell your friend in New York we've changed the name of our planetarium. We'll call it the New Hayden Planetarium." That shut the other fellow up completely.

Despite all that was going on with the museum, I managed to make a trip back to Alaska in the summer of 1949, directing a survey expedition on Mount McKinley for the Office of Naval Research. Part of the idea was to find a safer route to the top than via the lengthy Muldrow Glacier. (That was while the Navy still had some interest in cosmic ray research.) We made the very first helicopter landings on the northern approach to McKinley, near McGonagall Pass.

While in Alaska, I stopped in Fairbanks, and when I visited the University of Alaska Fairbanks, two of the pioneer McKinley

Conferring with my secretary, Mary Morgan, in my office.

climbers were there: Harry Karstens, who reached the summit with Hudson Stuck in 1913, and Charles McGonagall, who was a member of the Sourdough Expedition of 1910. Karstens, McGonagall, Terry Moore, and I posed for some pictures—it was a once-in-a-lifetime meeting, and there was a lot of Mount McKinley history in those photographs.

Our party posed on August 14, 1949, with an ancient Sikorsky H5G at the Wonder Lake Ranger Cabin. From left is Jim Gale, me, pilot Lieutenant Bill Weed, and crew chief Sergeant Sim Linebaugh. Jim was an experienced climber and good friend who joined me on many climbs, including Operation White Tower in the spring of 1947.

CHAPTER TWENTY

PIONEERING MOUNT MCKINLEY'S WEST BUTTRESS

Virtually all first ascents were made by what seemed to be the shortest and easiest route. For some time, however, I had been telling people that Mount McKinley had not been climbed by its easiest route. One day, Henry Hall—a prominent leader in the American Alpine Club, who lived in Cambridge, Massachusetts—said to me, "You know, this is crazy. You're saying that the side of the mountain that has never been climbed is shorter, safer, and easier than the route that has been climbed." I said, "Henry, the West Buttress route up Mount McKinley will soon be proved to be not only the shortest route up Mount McKinley, but also the safest and easiest."

Hardly anybody believed me. Some people said, "Brad Washburn's done pretty well up to this point, but what he has been saying is ridiculous." There were people who said I was going to ruin my reputation, and that we might even get killed on this new route up McKinley. The mountain had been climbed several more times by 1951, and always via the Muldrow Glacier. People knew that mountains were always climbed first by the easiest way. I said, "This is going to be different."

I knew that the West Buttress would almost certainly be the easiest way to climb Mount McKinley for a couple of reasons. First of all, I had been to the summit, and had seen the upper part of the route, looking down from Denali Pass. Second, I had made many aerial photographs that showed the details of the best route to follow. When Henry Buchtel from Denver wrote to say that he was going to try to make the first ascent by this route with four friends, I immediately asked if he would add Bill Hackett, Jim Gale, and me to his party. When we got there, it worked out that I was leading, because it was my route. And Jim Gale knew a helluva lot more about the mountain than the others, too, because he had been working with me over the years.

The climb began in mid-May of 1951, when I flew to Denver. Jim, Bill, and I had climbed together on McKinley in 1947; Henry brought John Ambler, Melvin Griffiths, Jerry More, and Barry Bishop from Denver. (Barry was one of the first Americans to climb Mount Everest, more than a decade later, and worked for the National Geographic Society for many years.)

We had the use of a Super Cub airplane that would land us on the Kahiltna Glacier at 7,000 feet, so we wouldn't have to make a long approach hike, or use a dog team to ferry supplies.

The fact that I was a pilot made it easier to predict the best place to land on the glacier, and I had Terry Moore, an accomplished mountaineer, as my pilot.

We left the little Chelatna airstrip, at about 1,200 feet, early in the day, changing into our woolly underwear right on the spot (since there wasn't a girl within forty miles in any direction). Terry had special hydraulically activated landing gear attached to the wheels. Using a device in the cockpit, he could speedily pump the skis up or down, so the airplane could land easily on a runway or on a glacier.

After 5:00 P.M., Terry and I flew around seeking to establish a beachhead on the mountain. We swung up the now-familiar,

During the 1951 climb, Don Sheldon, Alaska's most famous Bush pilot, paused in Talkeetna for a shot with my surveying gear.

rock-covered part of the Kahiltna Glacier. You couldn't even land a helicopter in those godforsaken piles of rocky ice. Some of the boulders were as big as a bungalow. As we climbed, we kept picking spots where we could land in an emergency; there were a lot above 4,000 feet, but few below that.

We pressed ahead to our 7,500-foot landing area above the last icefall, right at the bottom of McKinley. We skimmed over the lower part of it, huge, yawning crevasses below us as we crossed the crest of the icefall. There was no sun on the area where I wanted to land, and it was virtually impossible to gauge the altitude without shadows, so we went four miles downglacier and circled for twenty-five minutes, taking a look at our landing spot every five or six minutes.

At exactly 6:00, a thin streak of sun hit the spot where we wanted to land and we pounced on it, landing immediately, and perfectly, without even a bounce. The weather was so unpredictable, with dozens of different layers of mist both above and below us, that Terry didn't stay long, and both of us kept a constant watch on the small black hole down the Kahiltna Valley, which was his only route of return to the outer world.

We had quite a time getting the plane turned around, as the slush was very deep, and the crust not even thick enough to support a footstep. But we eventually heaved and pulled and headed the plane across the slope. Terry got aboard at 6:30, and took off down the 15 percent grade without the slightest trouble. I walked down his tracks and found that he had taken just 350 feet to get into the air. After an hour of work in the lonely silence of the vast, fog-draped basin, I had a flat tent platform stamped out and my 7 x 7 Logan tent up, radio inside, and ready for occupancy.

Terry returned a couple of hours later with supplies, but conditions were marginal, so I marked a four-hundred-foot runway with snowshoes and a duffle bag to help his depth perception. I stood at the upper end in front of the tent. He made a very nice landing, considering the abominable conditions—just one bounce.

At the end of the day, I was camped alone at 7,650 feet on the Kahiltna Glacier, exactly where we wanted to be, and only three and a half miles below Kahiltna Pass. It was totally calm, so quiet that you could hear your heart beat (as long as the stove was off). My God, what a good feeling it was to be there, after all of the hoping and planning!

On the 20th, a radio report informed me that Terry, who by then was president of the University of Alaska's Fairbanks campus, was unavoidably detained on school business, and his arrival with several of the other members of the party was uncertain. (Terry was held up because he had to have a conference with the chairman of the Board of Regents, to prepare a special report for the Congressional Un-American Activities Committee about a student prank that involved raising a Communist flag at commencement. What utter rot!) Bless his heart, Terry had his meeting, then flew in Bill Hackett, Jim Gale, and all of the rest of our gear by early evening.

June 21, the longest day of the year and my daughter's birthday, Terry flew me around to shoot some movies, then dropped me a mile and three-quarters up the trail at 8,000 feet. We moved everything up to that point, and kept going all day to establish a camp at 10,000 feet. It was a long climb, and we spent an hour pitching the tent—we had to dig through thirty inches of powder snow to get a firm crust base.

The next day was clear and calm with a temperature of 36 degrees that felt like scorching weather, and an Air Force C-47 made a supply drop. They heaved out a little over a ton of stuff in forty-three different pieces, most free fall, but some with parachutes. Augie Hiebert of KENI in Anchorage, the pioneer Alaska broadcaster, tape-recorded a fifteen-minute interview with us from the plane. We stamped out a thousand-foot landing field, thirty feet wide for Terry; dinner was frozen fried chicken, with fresh strawberries for dessert.

On June 25, Terry landed twice at the 10,000-foot camp—that broke Bob Reeve's old Lucania record for a high aircraft landing in Alaska. All the time we were climbing, I was working on my ongoing Mount McKinley survey. The most important survey station was at the 12,535-foot top of Kahiltna Dome; we constructed an igloo there for protection against bad weather—and needed it!

One thing that differentiated my visits to Mount McKinley from today's climbs is the amount of time we spent on the peak. Modern guides and citizen adventurers are on a timetable, with McKinley trips scheduled for three weeks. We

I was convinced that the West Buttress route was the easiest way to climb Mount McKinley, and our party proved it on July 10, 1951. Here, Jim Gale leads Bill Hackett as they tackle the last quarter-mile of the summit. I tarried behind a bit to take this picture at 5:00 P.M.

were never in so much of a hurry that we were forced to climb in really bad weather; we could duck inside a tent or an igloo when a storm hit.

Of course, if we had stayed in the tent the whole time that the weather was poor on McKinley, we would never have gotten anything done. So there were times we simply got caught out. On July 1, when we all took a load up to 12,000 feet, an hour below the next campsite, we had fog and snow and a light westerly breeze and didn't see a thing. It was terribly wet and warm all the way.

One thing about McKinley in the summer is that when it is clear, it is almost never really dark. You are so far north that the sun only dips below the horizon for a few minutes around midnight. July 2 was like that: the sunset never stopped. By 1:30 A.M., the sun was rising again, just to the left of Chitsia Mountain, flooding the whole sea of clouds and all the peaks with rose and silver. We also completed the survey work on Kahiltna Dome that day. It's the sort of job that must be done at night at that altitude, in the summer, to secure the most accurate survey data.

Such good weather on McKinley can never be counted on to last, and three days later, at 13,200 feet, we were blasted by a fiendish blizzard. The wind was blowing with gusts up to 60 mph, and it was snowing like hell. We decided to call the spot Windy Corner, and the name has stuck over the years.

Moving up the mountain on the 7th, Jim Gale and I made it to our 14,000-foot cache, and then tackled the slope up to the West Buttress with rough-locked snowshoes. The snow was abominable, deep and loose, but the thin layers of crust would hold with snowshoes (we would sink to our waists if we took them off). We finally wound up shoveling a trail for the last two hours, until we staggered, hot and exhausted, into the hollow underneath the 15,500-foot bergschrund. It was 2:45 P.M., and we were sure that we would never make the 16,000-foot shoulder we had as our goal for the day.

After some tea, however, we tackled the slope above the schrund, and chopped steps steadily till 7:00, in the most wretched snow imaginable. There was thin crust on top (for which we needed crampons), then granular snow for a few inches, then two thin layers of blue ice with powder in between. It took twenty or thirty chops per step. We clambered up steep granite on crampons at 7:15, and actually got above our 16,000-foot shoulder. We retreated to the schrund, spent two hours building an igloo, and had supper at 10:45. We were making headway, but it was slow and tough.

The next day, we did not leave camp until 12:30 P.M. Then we carried three light loads, and finished putting fixed ropes up the entire slope to 16,000 feet. This required about eight hundred feet of fixed rope, and five hundred feet of very steep climbing. The views of the Kahiltna Glacier, Mount Foraker, and Mount Hunter were stunning all day, in every conceivable combination of light and shadow.

It had often been said that the key to this climb, on this route, would be the next thousand feet to the 17,200-foot plateau. It succumbed to us in exactly an hour and forty minutes: we scrambled on rock and snow that was well packed by the wind, and had marvelous views to the west and south the whole time. We reached the crest of the plateau at 6:00, had a look up at Denali Pass, right in front of us, temptingly close. We were at the very top of the West Buttress of McKinley, and all that remained of new territory was the last, steep, thousand-foot slope up to the pass.

The next night, July 9, we camped in gorgeous blue skies above a silvery sea of clouds in the snow basin right below 18,000-foot Denali Pass, which seemed but a stone's throw away. Our objective was very nearly won; a single clear day and we would make the Pass.

To reach that spot, we put on our felt boots for the first time—they were a godsend. We left the igloo at 15,500 feet, and took an hour and a half to make the ridge. I had to cut a lot of new steps, because the fixed ropes had been shifted. The temperature was a warm 20 degrees, but there was a 30 mph breeze from the southwest. We reached the 17,000-foot cache in early afternoon, and couldn't see a hundred feet in front of us. The rocks were all covered with beautiful frost feathers.

We rose at 8:00 A.M. on July 10; it was clear, but there was a southwest lenticular cloud forming over the mountain. (We always called that cloud "altocumulus lenticularis sonofabitchicus"!) After breakfast, we decided to mark out a route to Denali Pass. It looked pretty icy in spots, but I was sure we would make it if the weather gave us a break.

When we left camp we were equipped for anything from taking a crack at Denali Pass to going all the way to the summit. It was 20 degrees and calm as we tackled the steep western slope of Denali Pass, the last unknown in our new route up Mount McKinley. The sastrugi were enormous—how the westerly winds must have howled across that bleak slope, both in summer and winter!

The going was never really steep, and the hard, icy snow and sastrugi alternated with breakable wind crust over ice. Jim, Bill, and I swung clear of a few crevasses and schrunds, and wound beneath two beautiful chunks of ice. We took lots of pictures and climbed very slowly, reaching the Pass safely at 12:15 P.M. It had taken us only two hours. We shook hands heartily at the conclusion of the first ascent of McKinley's West Buttress; anything more that we did now was pure frosting on the cake, on ground well known to all three of us.

At 1:00 P.M., we decided we would make a try for the summit, and at least get the trail marked for a distance upward. There were still cloud plumes over the North and South peaks, but there wasn't much wind. The clouds were down to 19,000 feet when we started.

We climbed up the ridge, as we had in 1947; much to our amazement, we ran into lots of our old trail markers. They had all been broken off nearly flush with the icy surface of the snow. My guess is that they had become loaded with frost, and the added resistance was enough for the wind to snap them. We found markers at intervals all the way to the top.

At 19,000 feet we went into the fog and the breeze got brisker, so I cut off to the left of our old route, keeping in the lee and heading for the hollow between the 19,200-foot dome and the summit. Jim and Bill were having a bit of a hard time with the altitude, so I picked up all of the trail markers, and carried my heavy Speed Graphic camera, too. It was the only time I had ever seen Jim really tired. Curiously, I had never felt better, even though I was forty-one years old, and was carrying forty pounds of camera gear and film. The weight seemed not to bother me a bit that afternoon.

We stopped for a forty-minute lunch in the dense fog and warm sun in the lee of the 19,200-foot shoulder, and then wallowed through knee-deep snow for fifteen minutes to swing back to the shoulder to look at the weather. It was perfect everywhere but on McKinley. As the gusts of wind blew the summit plume back, we could clearly see that even Mount Foraker didn't have a cloud on top. This sign made me sure that if we continued slowly upward, by 4:30 or 5:00 P.M., when it began to cool off, everything would clear.

It was a good theory, and at 4:30, as we were toiling up the summit cone amidst huge sastrugi, it really began to clear off and the top appeared above us through the mist. Our entire approach to the summit above 19,000 feet had been blind up to that point. We had used a detailed knowledge of the mountain, and trail markers laid out to literally survey us in a straight line. I set the course, and Jim or Bill would yell when I swung either way out of a straight line in the dense fog.

At about 19,800 feet I decided to strike to the right and try a slightly new route, right over the top of the Kahiltna Shoulder, to avoid a lot of half-hardened sastrugi. At 4:45 the weather really cleared as we reached the crest of the shoulder— the first people, I believe, ever to go there. The bamboo pole that we had left on the top in 1947 was still there, only about three hundred yards above us.

I unroped, and Jim and Bill went ahead so that I could get pictures of them as they approached the peak along that superb final ridge. The wind dropped to 10–15 mph as I loaded film with numb fingers.

I caught up to the others atop the last big hump on the ridge, a hundred yards short of the top, and broke the trail to the peak. I was totally overcome with emotion when, at 5:30, we slowly reached the summit of the final drift, and that whole amazing panorama to the east burst upon us. I hadn't really dreamed we would make it to the top that day.

We busily set to work to make a good series of movies and stills of both the summit itself, and the view. It was very cold work on the hands, and my fingers grew slightly numb from the exposure of changing film and focusing. The feeling lasted for hours. Forty-five minutes went by all too fast, and then we were ready to leave. The wind was coming up, and it was late in the day. Although the sun was shining brightly, its warmth was gone. Gusts of southwest wind of 30–40 mph cut like knives, and we began to shiver uncontrollably.

Yet we hated to leave. The view was so marvelous, clear in every direction: Mount Hayes, the Coast Range, Marcus Baker, Lake Minchumina, and lakes and mountain ranges that seemed hundreds of miles beyond to the northwest. Looking out at 100,000 square miles of Alaska in one sweep on a clear day is a thrilling experience; Anchorage is only 140 miles away, and you can see a good deal south of that.

At 6:15 we retied the bit of orange bunting we had left behind on the pole in 1947 with a new knot, and reluctantly bade farewell to the top. Twice before, upon leaving the summit, I had been convinced I would not return. Later that night, Jim Gale and I both mentioned that as we left the summit to begin our descent, we had tears trickling down our cheeks. Jim was not the kind of guy who would cry. He was a top sergeant, and top sergeants are hard-boiled, confident, tough. But we had been on the summit a couple of times, and both felt we would not be there again. We were right. I had never felt that way on any other mountain. We were saying good-bye to an old friend. This one was very special.

And so my predictions came true. The West Buttress route is the best way to climb Mount McKinley, and today, when mountaineering has exploded as an activity, something like 1,300 people try to climb it each spring. And most of them try to reach the summit via the West Buttress. We had an airplane available to us, something that none of the early pioneers had at their service; even today, if climbers weren't flown to the Kahiltna Glacier to start with, only 10 percent of them would make it to the top.

I wouldn't discourage anybody from going, but if you're going to go, you'd better be very comfortable with deep cold; big wind; and frequent, violent storms. The trouble with the West Buttress route is that it is technically easy enough that an

awful lot of people who try it are ill equipped. Their equipment or inexperience makes them fail, rather than the route
itself (which is a cinch, from a mountaineering standpoint).

But the truth is that McKinley is never easy. It is a big, cold
thing, and it can be a vicious enemy if you're not awfully careful. Some people call it a "walk-up," but that doesn't give the
mountain enough respect. Every year people are killed on it.

In the years since, I have flown over or past Mount
McKinley many times; it is not the same as being on it. On the
other hand, it's nice to reminisce and say, "Gee, that's where
we had a camp, and here's where we had the big snowstorm."

By 1951, Mount McKinley meant more to me than any
other mountains I had ever climbed, but I could never have
imagined that more than fifty years later it would continue to
play a role in my life. My links to Mount McKinley have stayed
alive through photography, mapmaking, and all of the young
people who ask me for advice.

I'd give anything to do it again tomorrow.

Chapter Twenty-One

MAPPING MCKINLEY

The same year that I climbed McKinley's West Buttress, I published *Mount McKinley and the Alaska Range in Literature,* the most complete bibliography of McKinley available. I was interested in getting a book out that would make it easy for other people interested in the mountain to find related subjects. Also, at that time, a photograph of mine was chosen as one of the best photographs from the first fifteen years of *Life* magazine, and displayed at the Museum of Modern Art in New York, and I was awarded an honorary Ph.D. from the University of Alaska.

That year, too, I was awarded the Distinguished Service Certificate by the Cambridge, Massachusetts Chamber of Commerce. It read, in part: "In recognition of the distinction which he has brought to his native city of Cambridge through his outstanding achievement in the scientific exploration of Alaskan Mountains and Glaciers. In gratitude for his determined devotion which at last is translating his vision of a popular science center for all New England into the new Museum of Science at Science Park, located in part in the City of Cambridge."

For decades, my life straddled two worlds, inside and outside of Alaska. Someone once asked me how my obituary would be written, and I said there would have to be two very different obituaries for the two places. Someone else once wrote that Barbara and I were the most famous Alaskans who had never lived in Alaska.

After I made the West Buttress climb, I was keenly interested in finalizing a map of Mount McKinley. My surveying work was not complete after the 1951 climb, and in 1953 I returned to obtain more data so that the map could be finished. In the course of completing the mapping work, I made the second ascent of Scott Peak (8,828 feet) on June 26, the second ascent of Mount Brooks (11,940 feet) on July 19, and the third ascent of Scott Peak, by a new route from the Sunset Glacier, on July 23. This was not a true mountaineering expedition, but had its focus on survey work. Chauncey "Chan" Waldron, Edward "Ned" Ames, and Barbara accompanied me. She and I were able to go to Alaska together again because the kids were in summer camp.

I departed from Massachusetts for my twentieth trip to Alaska on June 2, 1953, almost immediately after hearing that Mount Everest had at last been conquered, by Sir Edmund Hillary and Sherpa Tenzing Norgay, on May 29, the same day as the crowning of Queen Elizabeth II of England. It was electrifying news.

I reached McKinley Park on June 7, my forty-third birthday—so many of my birthdays at this stage of my life were celebrated in Alaska. This time, however, nobody with me knew about it. The next day I drove out to Teklanika, where the government survey had its advanced camp, with two helicopters and two Cub airplanes. After lunch, pilot Knute Bergh and I took a two-hour flight in gorgeous weather, and inspected both Scott Peak and the Brooks–Silverthrone area. It was a lovely flight and the view of McKinley, all clear above a 9,000-foot sea of clouds, was terrific. I could see that we couldn't land on top of Scott Peak, but I thought we would be able to land a helicopter about fifteen hundred feet below the top on the southwest side.

A few days later, the rest of the group arrived on the noon train from Fairbanks, and we spent the afternoon getting our automobile off a flatcar. It was wonderful to see everyone. Then, at 9:00 P.M., just as we were going to bed, we got the news that there had been a serious plane crash in the western part of the Park. An hour later it was confirmed that the plane was the same Super Cub in which I had flown two days earlier. Knute Bergh and Lt. Scott had been killed instantly at Stony Creek while trying to check out a new landing spot. Apparently they had caught their left wing in some low bushes and smashed into a cutbank, totally demolishing the plane. They must have been flying way too low. It was a tragic and unnecessary warning not to make steep turns near the ground.

Grant Pearson and Howard Cole went to investigate the wreck and bring the bodies back to Park headquarters. We woke at 5:00 A.M., when Howard returned, and I spent four rather morbid hours watching the bodies at the airport while the other fellows slept. At noon they took them to Anchorage by air, and Chan, Ned, and I drove out to Wonder Lake.

The first half of the drive was lovely, with lots of blue sky and cumulus clouds, but when we reached the scene of the crash at Stony Creek it began to drizzle and rained the rest of the way. The crash had certainly been terrific; the plane was a total wreck. They had hit the cutbank squarely, and scarcely moved an inch from the point of impact.

At Wonder Lake we got one brief glimpse of McKinley, towering far up into the evening light, and looking even higher than ever—a majestic sight. The next day our equipment arrived, and we had it about half-arranged when we decided to drive out for another look at McKinley. We got a perfect view of

Wickersham Wall, the extraordinary North Face of Mount McKinley, is one of the world's two greatest walls, equaled only by the Diamir Face of Nanga Parbat in the Himalaya. When, in 1903, Judge James Wickersham first saw it, he declared that nobody would ever get up it "except in a flying-machine"! This side of McKinley has been climbed less than a half-dozen times.

it. By June 14 we had all of our supplies sorted at Wonder Lake, and a government survey truck took most of our stuff to Camp Eielson. On our drive we stopped at Igloo Creek camp to say hello to Adolph Murie, the famous naturalist, and his family.

Soon we were camped at 5,600 feet on Scott Peak in a driving rainstorm. We expected snow next. The helicopters, piloted by Bill Kummer and Harold Stephenson, arrived at 6:50 P.M., right on schedule. We marked out a good landing area with strips of red cloth about half a mile east of Camp Eielson.

Once in the helicopters, we climbed rapidly up the valley of Sunrise Glacier and in ten minutes were at 6,000 feet. The weather was rapidly fouling to the west and it looked as if I might stand a chance of being stranded if they left me at the 7,500-foot landing strip, so we quickly changed plans.

We landed on the little pass on the east fork, on the north side of Scott Peak. Bill didn't even slow down his engine. I grabbed my baggage out of the plywood boxes on each side of the copter, and he was off four minutes after we landed. Then Harold set down and was off in three minutes. I felt really quite lonely, as it looked as if the clouds might really roll in before a third load arrived. But those pilots worked hard, making quick drops. Chauncey came in as the weather held on.

The first day that I had gone out with one of the pilots, we had landed on the Muldrow Glacier at around 7,500 feet with no trouble at all. On the way home, I had said to this fellow, "I think you've done this many times before. What do you do if your motor quits?" And he said, "I'll show you!" He just turned the switch that cut the motor, and we made a succession of very steep, descending spirals. When we were right near the ground he pulled back on the stick, which sped up the rotor, and we settled quietly onto the ground. You wouldn't even have known we had been in the air!

For nine days, we were pinned down at camp during a big storm. We spent our time cooking and playing spelling games. Barbara even regurgitated lectures from her days at Smith College. On June 26, we woke at 3:15 a.m. and marveled at how huge McKinley looked. We took off for Scott Peak at 5:10 a.m., and made excellent headway along the ridges. Amazing changes had taken place since the storm: masses of snow had melted away, and the snow ridge we had walked on the first trip had turned to dry shale. We reached the col and saw the darnedest sets of mountain sheep tracks. They were paired evenly and looked like circles, with each track about as big as your fist and each about two feet apart. How they got there heaven only knows, since there are bad icefalls below on either side.

The snow was "corn" on top of black ice; apparently it had rained right to the top in the big storm. But we found our little cache from the last trip in the 8,000-foot pass, and it was dry.

The climbing on Scott Peak was dreadful; every rock was rickety. Whole ledges tumbled away at the touch, and we had to advance extremely carefully, both on the rotten rock and on the ice and short slopes between the rock ribs. The first half of the climb from the col took only an hour, but it took two more hours to get the last four hundred vertical feet.

Once atop Scott Peak, the cool east breeze stopped abruptly, and it was calm and boiling hot in the sun. We had my heavy Wild T-3 theodolite with us, but not the tripod, so we went back down to get it. At 1:30 p.m., we got the theodolite raised and started to work at once, but it was a losing battle. We just couldn't use the marker, it was so hazy. We learned on the radio that it was a record 91 degrees in Talkeetna.

We left the top at 5:30, and had a hellish time getting down the ropes without braining each other with loose rocks. On the way down, I collected some lichens and moss at 8,000 feet, the highest I had ever seen them in the Alaska Range.

On July 19, we climbed Mount Brooks to put in a key survey station at its top. (We had tried once before, but failed to reach the summit because of terrible snow conditions.) We rose at 3:00 A.M. to discover unsettled weather. There were seas of clouds above and below us, so we went back to sleep until 7:30. Then we started climbing through dense clouds, and had a good deal of trouble finding our old trail above 9,000 feet because it was all drifted over.

But the willow wands did a wonderful job for us, and we found our way through to the 10,500-foot cache we'd previously put in. We walked in wet, drizzly snow that melted the second it touched you. My warm woolen pants had been left behind at the hotel, and my light, twill pants soaked up water like a sponge. They were dripping, but fortunately my rather experimental boots were dry, except from sweat, and marvelously comfortable.

The going ahead was awful—dry powder with slush underneath, so deep that an ice axe wouldn't touch bottom. Ned and I, taking turns at the job, broke trail to the top of the last big cornice on the ridge at 11,000 feet, where it leveled out before the final climb.

Everybody and everything was soaking wet when we paused for lunch. Then we resumed climbing in dense fog, with sun breaking through at intervals. When we reached the lower peak, we still couldn't see the top, but kept plowing on. I left my load of about forty pounds at 11,200 feet, because it was terribly slow both breaking and packing at the same time.

Finally, just before 6:00 P.M., we reached the top of Mount Brooks, after topping two false summits, one of which really fooled us. The clouds were blowing gently over the top. My, what a view!

We decided to risk a bivouac on the top, on the assumption that it would stay clear overnight and we could accomplish considerable survey work. The top was very different from what I had expected. A nice, flat-topped dome supported by vertical slate ledges to the southwest, it proved to be an excellent place for a camp. The snow was dry and hard, so we built a nice snow-cave camp and set up my theodolite.

We were very uncomfortable that night due to the extreme cold, and got up at 2:20 A.M., when the sun touched the top of McKinley—it was one of the most beautiful sunrises I've ever seen. We surveyed continuously until 9:00 A.M., except for fifteen minutes for breakfast. In mid-afternoon a sight-seeing plane appeared, and we flashed them with my signaling mirror. The plane made two swoops right over camp, and I am sure they were surprised to see anyone up there.

The top of Mount Brooks is ten or so miles from McKinley, and when we looked through the high-powered telescope of my theodolite, we were able to see the bamboo pole that we had left on the summit in 1951. The cloth we had tied to the pole was still flapping in the wind.

The map of McKinley came out in 1960, when I was fifty. I had spent years doing the surveys that led to the completion of my map, and I ended up working with the Swiss to print it. Through a woman I knew named Stephanie Martin, I met Ernst Feuz, who was from a famous Swiss family of high-mountain guides. Ernst managed Neue Warenhaus, the Sears Roebuck of Switzerland. Through Ernst I met Karl Weber, the president of Neue Warenhaus. He, in turn, introduced me to the leading people at Landestopographie in Wabern, on the outskirts of Bern, where the best maps in the world are made and printed.

A Map of
Mount McKinley
Alaska

My map of Mount McKinley was published in 1960, when I was fifty years old, printed in Switzerland by the Swiss Federal Institute of Topography.

They agreed to make and print my map of Mount McKinley, and that was the first time the Swiss officials had printed a map on any subject outside Switzerland. The Swiss are watchmakers and watchmakers do everything with precision. They love perfection. I'm a perfectionist, and I like working with perfectionists.

I never made another large-scale Alaska mountain climb. There were no more first ascents to try, and the surveying was complete, so I didn't have good reasons to go to those high points anymore. There were new challenges ahead in different parts of my life.

Our children, Teddy, Dotty, and Betsy, in 1949. Our cross-country drive in the summer of '55 was an unforgettable road show, and we hit some of the best vacation sites in America, from Niagara Falls, to Lincoln's Tomb, the Grand Canyon, Las Vegas, and a new thing called Disneyland.

CHAPTER TWENTY-TWO

EXPLORING AMERICA
WITH OUR CHILDREN

For all of the adventures we've had together, one of the best trips Barbara and I ever took was driving across the United States with our three children in the summer of 1955. We left Boston on July 30 and returned on September 6. We logged many thousands of miles and gathered wonderful memories along a route that zigzagged all over the map. Then, when we reached the West Coast, we visited an exciting new tourist attraction that had just opened one month earlier: Disneyland. The best part was that Barbara and I were with the kids the whole time, which just didn't happen when we went to the mountains.

The temperature was in the high nineties as the Washburn family arrived in Detroit, completing the first leg of the journey: through upstate New York, Niagara Falls, Ontario, and into Michigan. There we were to pick up a brand-new Plymouth Suburban with power steering and an automatic gearshift—both firsts for me—from a friend at the Chrysler Corporation, with the assignment of delivering the fancy new car to a dealer in Los Angeles. Meanwhile another friend would return our old car to Boston. I was given instructions to treat the car very gently for 300 miles or so and only traveled 143 miles the first day.

Barbara and I wanted the kids to see as much of America as possible, and the entire trip was an adventure—for the adults, too. We'd envisioned that we would do a lot of camping, but it didn't take long for that plan to change. After an uncomfortable early night out, the children would have none of it. They preferred indoor beds, and television—another brand new marvel for all of us. We ended up spending a lot more money than we'd expected.

We took the Suburban through Indiana and into Illinois, with Teddy and I making a side trip to see a huge grain elevator at Gibson City. Then all of us visited Lincoln's Tomb, where it was nice and cool inside. Everywhere we went the temperature had been hovering around ninety-five degrees, hot as hell.

In Kansas City, we took a short swing through downtown, then stopped briefly in Emporia, Kansas, to see William Allen White's famous *Emporia Gazette* newspaper, then visited old friends in Wichita. We got a tour of the Coleman Company, makers of the well-known camp stoves and lanterns that we had used on so many of our trips, and even met Mr. W. C. Coleman himself. As we headed west, the children all bought cowboy hats in a curio shop; the Washburns looked like real dudes.

When we crossed into Colorado, it felt as if we'd truly entered the West. A sign marking a point of interest was at the boundary. It announced that we were on the Santa Fe Trail: "Here marched history." Setting out from Los Animas, we were surrounded by cactus and sagebrush. We also passed the Santa Fe Chief, which looked exactly like Teddy's toy model train. In Denver we relaxed by swimming in a community pool and visited their Museum of Natural History. All of us, except Betsy, drove to the top of 14,110-foot Pike's Peak and I noticed the road was much better than the primitive route up our Mount Washington. We were groggy on top for lack of oxygen.

Near Shiprock, New Mexico, we left the main road to take a desert trail, and bang! We hit a rock as big as a grapefruit. It knocked off the exhaust pipe and cracked the exhaust manifold. Luckily, a Plymouth dealer in Cortez took care of our problem. As if that wasn't enough, the next day, I pulled the biggest boner of the trip.

At 6:00 a.m., I was backing the car away from the motel without turning on the power. (I didn't want to wake up all of the other guests, so I'd planned to start it about fifty yards away.) I coasted right into a telephone pole! There was a sickening crash and the wires gyrated wildly above. The effort to maintain silence was a royal flop. Everyone looked out the windows to see what was happening. I was pretty certain we would not be able to open the back door for the rest of the trip; it wore a deep imprint of a telephone pole, and the beautiful chrome trim was sadly mashed. The only ill effect it had on the driving was to put the chief driver into complete disgrace.

For me, the Grand Canyon was one of our most important goals of the trip, and seeing the place brought back so many memories. My family had toured the area when I was a boy in 1916; this was my first time back. I remembered how my older sister went off to hike the Bright Angel Trail without telling anybody. She just disappeared, and we could do nothing but wait patiently. Looking around the Bright Angel Lodge area in 1955, little seemed to have changed. Of course, in the future, Barbara and I would make many trips back to the Grand Canyon to map it.

We tried to make reservations for a muleback ride down the Canyon, but they wouldn't take anyone under twelve, ruling out Betsy. They thought the trip was too long and too hot for young ones. But we all signed up anyway and just hoped that when it was time to ride the next day, we could find a nice guide who would let her go. That afternoon, we drove along the edge of the Canyon to Hermit's Rest. It was the same old building with a huge fireplace that I recalled.

The next day, Barbara and I rose to take pictures of the magnificent canyon in the early light. Later the children took a two-hour horseback ride through the forest along the edge of the canyon. As for the mule ride, we finally decided that Betsy and I would get a head start and walk down while the others rode. It would have been heartbreaking not to have her go with us. So Barbara and I gathered food, flashlight batteries, and fruit juice, and made up two packs.

Betsy and I started down the Kaibab Trail at 4:30 on a perfect, clear afternoon. The others watched from the edge of the cliff and waved until we disappeared around one of the buttresses. My daughter's pack wound up on top of mine within a half an hour. Our original plan was to spend the night partway down, but we made such good time that we decided to go all of the way to the Phantom Ranch at the bottom. The trail was hot underfoot, a sort of sandy powder ground up by the mules' hoofs and heated all day by the sun. We took the precaution of binding our feet with adhesive tape, so neither of us had even a tiny blister.

Betsy and I rested fairly frequently and had wee sips from our two small thermos bottles. The sun set just as we headed down into the gorge, and it was dusk when we reached the suspension bridge across the Colorado River. Going through a short tunnel hewn through the rocks was weird in the eerie light cast by our flashlights.

I wish we had brought a lot of extra adhesive tape. We could have sold it for a dollar a yard to the people who arrived at the ranch on foot with ghastly blisters. The next day, we greeted the rest of the family. No blisters there, but they were pretty saddle-sore and tender after a five-hour mule ride.

Later, while we were all by the pool, a small, yellow scorpion landed on my stomach and bit me, but I managed to flick it off quickly. We captured it in a bottle and decided to bring it with us.

The next morning, Barbara, Dotty, and Teddy hit the trail at 8:00 a.m. As it turned out, Betsy and I didn't have to walk back—we hitched mule rides up with Jay Goza, a packer who carried supplies to the ranch; he was not bound by the general mule regulations. Jay rested the mules every fifteen minutes or so, but we only dismounted once during the whole climb out. We passed the others about an hour below the rim, where they were resting. Back at the top, my scorpion caused quite a stir. I was amazed to read what a miserable time I might have had if its bite had really had its proper effect on me: nausea, cramps, convulsions, maybe even death. (Teddy joked that I easily could scare any scorpion to death.)

Leaving the Grand Canyon, we piled back into the car and headed for the Pacific Coast, stopping in Las Vegas (where, by losing at the slot machines, Barbara and I tried to show the kids that gambling did not pay). Onward we toured, with stops at the Hoover Dam, Death Valley, and Yosemite National Park. We had a reservation at the great photographer Ansel Adams's studio, then saw a conservation exhibition, where I was pleased and surprised to find two of my own pictures on display.

The grand opening of Disneyland one month earlier had gotten incredible publicity all over the country, and we were keenly looking forward to our visit on August 30. The kids were crazy about the place: the 1890s atmosphere, the horse-drawn cars, the old trains, a "trip to the moon" in a rocket ship, and the ride on Mark Twain's Mississippi River stern-wheeler. All of it was fabulous. The Matterhorn attraction wasn't part of the Disneyland skyline until 1959, so I didn't get to see that replica—at 1/100th the size of the real thing—of the mountain that I'd climbed at age sixteen.

That five-week trip in the summer of 1955 was one of the best in my life. By the time we turned the car in to the dealer, a little worse for the wear and tear, we had clocked 5,716 miles. They took one look at the dent from my unfortunate crash and asked, "How the hell did you do that?" I answered honestly, and since they still haven't charged me for it, I don't think they will.

CHAPTER TWENTY-THREE

TELLING EVERYTHING
ABOUT DR. FREDERICK A. COOK

In 1955, I began a field investigation into Dr. Frederick Cook's alleged first ascent of Mount McKinley. It was clear to me that there was no way Dr. Cook could have climbed McKinley when he said he did in 1906. I believed that his claim was a hoax, and I was surprised there were still follow- ers who believed that he had done it. The more I came to know about McKinley, the more I wanted to find out what Cook actually *did* do.

Belmore Browne was one of the first skeptics; he and Herschel Parker had climbed within three hundred vertical feet of the summit of McKinley in 1912—which would have been the first ascent—before being turned back by a storm. That first-hand knowledge of the mountain gave them the perspective to understand that Cook's claim that he had climbed McKinley in twelve days—eight days ascending and four descending—couldn't possibly be true. Browne said something wonderful: "Cook's claim could no more be true than if a New Yorker said he walked from the Brooklyn Bridge to Grant's Tomb in ten minutes." Ultimately, it seemed apparent that Cook had gone to McKinley to create newspaper excitement, so he could raise money for a trip to the North Pole. And it worked.

With others, I proved that Dr. Frederick Cook certainly did not climb to the summit of Mount McKinley; however, his descendents continue to defend his record. This view is looking southwest from the top of Stony Hill at Mile 62 on Alaska's Denali Highway.

Cook had been to McKinley before his supposed first ascent; he had gone in 1903, with the explorer Robert Dunn. Belmore later got to know Bob Dunn very well. In the mid-1950s I discovered, to my amazement, that Robert Dunn was still very much alive and living in Katonah, New York. I called him up, and somehow he knew all about Barbara and me, and eagerly invited us to drive down and spend the weekend with him.

We had a memorable weekend. Dunn turned out to be a crotchety old fellow, but very eager to talk about the past. He had lived a life of travel and exploration, making the first ascent of 14,000-foot Mount Wrangell in Alaska by dog team, visiting huge volcanoes in Kamchatka, and spending several months in 1903 on a pack-train circumnavigation of Mount McKinley.

After graduating from Harvard, Dunn started out as a reporter (for the famous editor Lincoln Steffens) at the *Commercial Advertiser* in New York. One day Cook showed up in the office trying to raise money for a possible first ascent of Mount McKinley. Steffens assigned Dunn to go to Alaska, follow the expedition, and write about it.

Cook still needed money, however. Dunn had a wealthy aunt named Anna Hunter, and she gave the expedition a $25,000 gift. Dunn got Mount Hunter in Alaska named for her—although, when he pulled out his original pictures from 1903 and showed Barbara and me a picture of what he said was the mountain, I pointed out that it was actually Peters Dome. (He got furious about that, until I reminded him that he had accurately described Hunter as the tallest mountain between McKinley and Foraker.)

The expedition made it about halfway up McKinley before completing a circumnavigation. Dunn wrote a book, *The Shameless Diary of an Explorer,* and it made Cook out to be something of a weird character. Dunn had observed that Cook made himself out to be a big scientific expert, but didn't know how to use the equipment. Still, Cook had insisted on posing for pictures with the equipment as if he knew what he was doing.

Dunn gave Barbara and me his precious original negative of Peters Dome, which I sent to the archives of the American Alpine Club. Back in Boston I told George Peabody Gardner, one of the Science Museum's key trustees, about our extraordinary visit. It turned out that Dunn had been his mother's first boyfriend!

At a subsequent dinner in Brookline, Massachusetts, Dunn, the Washburns, and the Gardners gathered. One thing we did was raise our glasses high in a toast to Dr. Frederick Albert Cook! (Dunn died a few years later and George Gardner's generous mother made a gift to the Museum of Science, which established the Robert Dunn Endowment Fund for exploration, travel, or the publication of books or maps on such subjects. The money from the Robert Dunn fund helped produce my Mount McKinley map, and later, provided the seed money for my Mount Everest map.)

Meeting Dunn at that time had been fortuitous. More and more, I had been thinking of trying to revisit the places Cook had talked about. In 1953, on a McKinley flight, I had pinned down the location of what came to be known as the "Fake Peak," the place where Cook actually stood when he claimed to be on the summit of McKinley. Anyone who knew anything about it knew that the footsteps in Cook's "summit" photograph had to have been made in soft, fluffy, low-altitude snow. At the summit of Mount McKinley, you couldn't make footsteps like that. Belmore Browne guessed right away that the photo must have been taken at around 5,000 feet; he was right on the button.

Famed Alaskan pilot Don Sheldon flew me in to Fake Peak once, and we found the rock and the campsite that Cook had used. The camp was twenty-four miles, and the Fake Peak was nineteen miles, from the summit of McKinley. We weren't so much angry as fascinated by the whole damned thing—it was a real detective story. By 1955, I thought we had proven the case that Cook had not done it. Later, we even found pictures in the Ohio State archives, where Cook's material ended up, that showed he had removed his tent from the picture so it might seem to be on McKinley.

When Cook came off the mountain, the first people he spoke to were members of the Mazamas mountaineering club of Portland, Oregon. In 1910, after the controversy got going, the club ran an expedition to McKinley to prove that Cook did it, at the same time that Belmore Browne went in to prove exactly the opposite. The Mazamas and Browne met on the Ruth Glacier, and agreed that Cook could never have done what he said. At the time, Cook was discredited by people who *thought* that he couldn't have done it, but they couldn't *prove* that he hadn't done it.

Forty-five years later, we had the evidence that showed conclusively that Cook had not done it. Nonetheless, decades after that, people were still insisting that he had. The Frederick Cook Society stayed very much alive because Cook's granddaughter, Janet Vetter, gave it lots of money. They had a trust in Florida as a nonprofit, charitable, educational institution, so they kept working at it. In the 1990s, when the Cook Society went to Alaska and hired guides and tried to prove again that Cook had made it, that stirred me up. There was a mock trial on the issue in Fairbanks, but the Cook Society people refused to participate. The "court" ruled that he had not climbed the mountain.

I was afraid that the mock trial would be a stupid waste of time because the Cook Society refused to be present. You can't have a trial if the defendant isn't there. I issued a challenge to the Cook Society, saying I would debate them any place they wished, but they didn't take me up on it. They wouldn't go anywhere near me.

At the time, I thought that the Cook Society was just waiting for me to die, as mine was the loudest voice in opposition. That's why I wrote *The Dishonorable Dr. Cook*. I wanted to present the case in complete form for future generations, so there would be no doubt that Cook was not the first to climb Mount McKinley.

It was clear that Cook didn't even want to climb McKinley. He was just convinced that the publicity would get him the money he needed to go to the North Pole. It worked flawlessly: he succeeded in getting all the money he needed, left for the Pole, and faked that exploration, too!

It may come as a surprise, but I would have loved to have met Dr. Cook before his death in 1940. I don't know what I would have said. I'm reminded of something Belmore Browne told me: one time he ran into Cook on a train, and told him that he had fooled a lot of people for a long time. Cook had just laughed at him.

Now the Cook Society has nothing to do.

CHAPTER TWENTY-FOUR

A GROWING MUSEUM AND THE BRADFORD WASHBURN AWARD

The building of Boston's Museum of Science was really my life's work. If I could be remembered for just one thing, I'd like it to be that I was the fellow who came up with the idea of building the Museum of Science, and built it. That museum is the one thing I did that the general public knew about, cared about, and was excited about. The public benefited from the museum; I don't think they benefited so much from my research on Dr. Cook. And only a relatively small number of people even knew that I had made a map of Mount McKinley.

In 1964, to celebrate my twenty-fifth year as director of the museum, the trustees established the Bradford Washburn Award. I later learned that Royal Little—a trustee, as well as a lifelong friend—had been the main force behind the project. The award, consisting of a gold medal and a sum of $10,000, is presented to "an individual who has made an outstanding contribution toward public understanding of science, its importance, its fascination, and the vital role it plays in all our lives."

The first recipients were author and teacher Thornton W. Burgess; geologist, teacher, and author Kirtley F. Mather; and Dr. Gilbert Grosvenor, founder and president of the National Geographic Society—because all of these special men had influenced my life substantially. Among the others who have

In 1960, Barbara and I celebrated two great occasions: we danced at our daughter Dotty's debutante cotillion, and the map of McKinley was published. Photo courtesy Bradford Bachrach.

received the award over the years are oceanographer Jacques-Yves Cousteau, Walter Cronkite, Dr. Jane Goodall, Arthur C. Clarke, Dr. Carl Sagan, Dr. Isaac Asimov, Dr. Mary D. Leakey, Dr. Roger Tory Peterson, Thor Heyderdahl, Stephen Jay Gould, and General Charles E. Yeager. In 1989, on the fiftieth anniversary of my having become the director of the museum, Barbara and I were honored with the award.

It's a helluva list of people, and I've met every one of them. Walter Cronkite is still a very good friend. I've always felt that Walter was a person of great quality—a little bit like Abraham Lincoln. I don't know anybody who disagrees with, or dislikes, Walter Cronkite. I don't choose the recipients, but I am an ex officio member of the selection committee. It's wonderful to have my name attached to such an award.

In a letter dated August 27, 1972, Charles Lindbergh wrote to me, explaining that he had to decline acceptance of the Bradford Washburn Award. In part, he wrote:

Ceremonies and awards involve an old and serious problem for us. On the one hand, we find ourselves deeply grateful; on the other, they are simply incompatible with the way of life we want to lead. We like to live quietly, to have time for our children and friends, and beyond that to concentrate on research, writing, and other interests. Formal functions are distracting and time-consuming to an extent that makes it impossible for us to cope with them in our framework of life.

I have written frankly in the hope that you may be able to understand our position. Let me thank you again for your consideration in writing, for the honor you have suggested, and for the confidence you have placed in us.

Sincerely, Charles A. Lindbergh

Few people around today can imagine what a hero Charles Lindbergh was when he became the first person to fly across the Atlantic Ocean in 1927.

A little more than a month later, on September 29, 1972, I wrote back to Lindbergh, saying, in part,

I have only just received your letter of a month ago, on my return from a mapping project at the Grand Canyon. As you can well imagine, we are extremely sorry that you cannot accept our award. Yet, having been through a microcosm of what you describe, I can well understand the feelings that brought you to this decision. I am very grateful for your thoughtful letter.

Someday I hope very much that our paths can cross, as we have a great many similar interests and friends in common.

Lindbergh was a curious guy, and I never did meet him. But the strangest thing is that no copy of the letter offering him that award has ever turned up in the museum files. I wonder if he was ever offered the Bradford Washburn Award! The museum has a copy of every other letter that's been sent offering the award. Perhaps the museum had just asked him to come and speak. The whole situation is weird.

My life was heavily focused on the museum, and some years passed without my visiting Alaska. By the end of the 1960s I was getting to be sixty years old. I had a wife and children. I had climbed all of the big peaks I expected to climb. You couldn't have beaten McKinley as a gorgeous experience in 1951. It was a great culmination of that part of my life.

But I do miss climbing.

In 1965, I went back to the mountains for an expedition in the Yukon Territory, to complete survey work on a map of Mount Kennedy. I didn't do any climbing on March 22, but we made the highest helicopter landing in Canada to that point, on the summit of Mount Hubbard, at 15,015 feet.

I was the field leader of the party, representing the

National Geographic Society. We had discovered the 13,869-foot peak on the Yukon Expedition of 1935, but it was renamed Mount Kennedy after JFK was assassinated in November 1963. There was a big fuss about who should be the first to climb Mount Kennedy. Of course Bobby Kennedy wanted to be part of it, and he went, and was indeed the first person to reach the top. Jim Whittaker, the first American to climb Mount Everest, was there as his guide.

I knew Jack Kennedy, but had never met Bobby. Flying into the mountains from Whitehorse, over this absolutely marvelous country, when he could have been looking out the window, he was reading a book. I think he was basically interested in politics.

Each year, I would get a nice telegram from Bobby Kennedy thanking me again for all that I had done to help on the trip. In May of 1968, when he was running for president, I got a telegram from Bobby saying, "I'm trying to climb a very high mountain again and wish you were here to help me to the top." That was my last contact with him.

National Geographic photographer Chuck O'Rear captured this photo of Barbara and me surveying atop Dana Butte in the middle of the Grand Canyon, September 2, 1972.

Chapter Twenty-Five

Mapping the Grand Canyon with Barbara

In 1971, I made two trips to the Grand Canyon to begin a mapping project with a $30,000 grant from the National Geographic Society. The plan was to map eighty square miles in what we called the "heart" of the Canyon. The next year I made three more trips, this time with Barbara, and received an additional National Geographic Society grant to extend the mapping to the North Rim and along the Canyon's eastern edge, covering a total area of 162 square miles. One of the great things about this project was Barbara's active involvement. She helped me every step of the way, and we were almost always together, even during scores of helicopter flights.

Many people associate Barbara and me with Mount McKinley and Alaska, but not too many people associate us with the Grand Canyon and Arizona. It was ironic in a sense, because this was the opposite extreme: instead of extremely cold and dry, it was extremely hot and dry. In 1971, the same year that I began the mapping, I published a small book called *A Tourist Guide to Mount McKinley*. Otherwise, I was pretty much removed from Alaska in those years—spending so much time in the Grand Canyon meant that I did not visit Alaska at all from 1969 to 1973.

Mapping the Grand Canyon.

I love distant horizons, and the Grand Canyon qualified
as much as McKinley did. I took photographs and made a map
of Mount McKinley so people could have the vicarious experience of making an ascent. I brought back mapping information from all my trips to make it easier for others to have the
same experiences. In its own way, mapping the Grand Canyon
was just as satisfying as climbing or flying over McKinley.

We made hundreds of helicopter landings in the canyon. Typically, I would be left on a butte or pinnacle with laser equipment, and she would set up the prisms that reflected the beam back to me. The laser measured the distance between us— a real miracle. After the readings were taken, Barbara and the helicopter would come back to pick me up. I'll never forget an experience that I had one day, on the top of one of these buttes. The top was a sandy little spot about the size of the 9-by-12 rug in our living room. I lay down in the hot sun, and it was so quiet that I could hear my own heart beat. I've never experienced such total silence anywhere else.

The Grand Canyon experience was quite different from

The most beautiful view of the Grand Canyon is from Hopi Point. It is only a short distance from a big hotel where hundreds of tourists stay. Every morning, when the weather is good, people get up to see the sunrise at Hopi Point. Then they go back to bed. Barbara and I would survey very early in the day, when almost nobody was there—we had to work at off times so people wouldn't disturb us with millions of questions.

Early one summer day, Barbara and I were at Hopi Point making a laser sight all the way to the bottom of the Canyon. We were outside the railing. A station wagon pulled up right behind us. Two young children, a boy and a girl, got out of the car and they danced up to the railing behind us. The little girl said, "Daddy, what on earth did they do with all of the stuff that they took out of this place?" I sent it as a joke to the New Yorker, *but they did not publish it. I think they thought it was too good to be true.*

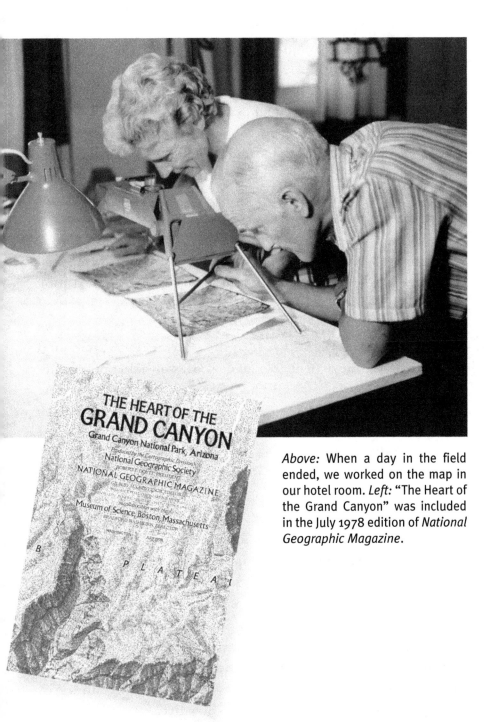

Above: When a day in the field ended, we worked on the map in our hotel room. *Left:* "The Heart of the Grand Canyon" was included in the July 1978 edition of *National Geographic Magazine.*

mapping in Alaska. Mapping technology was changing, and there was no expedition. Most of the time it was fun: Barbara and me, a helicopter pilot, and some prisms, at work in one of the wonders of the world. The best picture of Barbara and me at work was taken on this trip, when we were surveying on the very top of Dana Butte. I told the National Geographic Society that our work there would epitomize our efforts in the Canyon, and they sent photographer Chuck O'Rear, who shot the picture from a circling helicopter.

To make the map, we put in five seasons of fieldwork between 1971 and 1975, and two years of cartographic laboratory work in Washington, D.C. and Bern, Switzerland. It took so long because I couldn't get away as often, or stay as long as I had on my Alaska trips—the museum was growing larger. So we made a series of short forays into the canyon. Each time we'd map a little bit more of it. We made scores of helicopter landings on those pinnacles, and I became pretty much of an expert at working with the helicopter people on where we could or could not land. They would shoot me into some places that were so small that they couldn't set the helicopter down at all. They would land me on a tiny ledge and leave me to do the work, then pick me up later.

This was the last time that we used a big, heavy theodolite to measure angles, and a Laser Ranger instrument to measure distances. Our Grand Canyon map was developed out of thousands of laser distances and an equal number of angles. Later, when we mapped Mount Everest, we didn't use any angles at all, only scores of Global Positioning Satellite readings.

The *National Geographic* published our Grand Canyon map in July 1978. To my amazement, the Grand Canyon map is up on one of the walls in the Brookhaven retirement complex in Lexington, Massachusetts, where we now live.

CHAPTER TWENTY-SIX

INTO AFRICA

In January of 1973, Royal Little invited Barbara and me to go on a photographic safari to Africa. This came right after my busiest months of fund-raising for the museum, and I was completely worn out. I said to Barbara, "I just can't go. I'm absolutely exhausted." However, Barbara reacted quite effectively. She said, "If you don't want to go, I'm going to go anyway, alone, with Royal Little." I said, "For God's sake, be gentle. I've been absolutely battered fund-raising." Finally, under duress, I agreed to go, and it turned out to be the best trip that we ever took.

For one thing, we were together all of the time. And Royal Little, his son Arthur, and Arthur's wife were there. The guide, Sydney Downey, was fabulous—he had been the guide for the Queen of England on her African safari.

The trip started in February. On the way, to minimize jet lag, we flew to Europe and spent a few days relaxing in Greece. They ended up having the coldest night they had ever had in Athens and there was six inches of snow on the Acropolis. Then we flew directly to Nairobi, Kenya, where we met Roy Little, and continued on to Tanzania. It was a memorable trip because there was no work to do: it was a camera safari, and the animals did all the work.

One day, driving across a tremendous plain—no trees at all, just grass—it was hot and dry as hell. Downey said, "I want you to look ahead." We couldn't see anything. He handed over a pair of binoculars. "Don't you see the heat wave on the horizon?" We could see nothing but sky and dry grass. After a minute I said, "Yes, I can see some movement." It was not heat waves at all. There were hundreds of thousands of wildebeest moving at the edge of the horizon! This was the famous migration of the wildebeest.

I thought we would just sit in the vehicle, but we started moving. We drove forward, 3–4 mph, straight through that incredible herd. I'll never forget the sound of their grunting. But they paid no attention to us whatsoever: it was as if we didn't exist. They kept going, and we finally emerged on the other side of the herd.

Syd told us that he never turned the engine off while photographing wild animals. He said, "One time a huge rhino was very near us and we stopped to watch him. When we tried to start the Land Rover it didn't start fast enough, and the rhino put its horn right through the backseat." Two tourists were sitting in that seat and they couldn't stand up because the rhino's horn pinned them like a seat belt right across their laps! The rhino tried to back out, but its curved horn was stuck in the metal of the vehicle. They had a helluva time getting the auto disconnected from the rhino.

We saw all types of animals: lions, elephants, a leopard, hyenas, giraffes, millions of zebras. And we didn't have to make a map, and we didn't have to fill out a report. I had no responsibility at all; other people did all the managing. We slept in tents, and we had pretty close to forty people taking care of the five of us.

We got to within a hundred yards or so of several large lions who were up on a pile of rocks, and we got awfully close

I photographed the summit of Mount Kilimanjaro in February 1973, just before we flew down and right through this crater, well below Kili's summit, emerging safely in the upper right corner of this extraordinary aerial picture.

to a leopard hanging in a tree. Syd Downey was terrific; he knew where all of the animals were, and the best time of day to see them. It was a little bit like being with a top-notch guide on a mountain.

One thing Roy wanted very much to do was fly about four hundred miles to visit Jane Goodall, who was doing research on primates at the Gambe National Reserve, also in Tanzania. When the pilot who was going to fly us there arrived, he was too exhausted to take us because he had been doing rescue work all night; he wanted to rest for a day. Roy was frantic. Jane Goodall was expecting us, and in those days they didn't have any telephones or radios in the bush. He said, "Brad, you can fly, can't you?" The airplane wasn't like any I had ever flown, but we got the pilot to agree to take off, and let me take the controls. The pilot went to sleep, and I flew. Eventually, I nudged the pilot and said, "Wake up, we're at Kigoma. It's time to land." He woke up with a start and made a beautiful landing.

At Kigoma we took a small motorboat up the lake, and spent several days visiting Jane Goodall. Barbara, in particular, was fascinated by the behavior of the animals. Once, a baboon developed an inordinate fascination with Barbara. We had been told that if we encountered one of these animals to just stand still, and that if we tried to pet it, it might bite us. Barbara stood still, and the animal picked at her, her brightly colored skirt, looked her over, and then just walked away.

Of course, I couldn't go to East Africa, to Tanzania no less, and not take a look at Mount Kilimanjaro, at 19,340 feet the highest point in Africa. Almost as tall as Mount McKinley, it is not a glaciated peak, though it does have snow and ice around its top and in its crater. I asked Roy if the plane that was going to take us back to Nairobi could arrive an hour early so I could make a flight over the summit. The plane arrived at 7:00 A.M. on a cloudless, windless morning.

I explained to the pilot that I was also a pilot, and that I wanted to do something very special. We circled upward until we were a little above 20,000 feet, over Mawenzi, Kili's lower sister peak. We then aimed directly at the center of Kilimanjaro's crater and started our descent.

Thousands of years ago, when Kilimanjaro was young—like Mount St. Helens in Washington—it exploded. The eruption blew out the side, forming a U-shaped crater with an open end. We flew right down through the crater, emerging safely on the other side. And I got a couple of gorgeous photographs of the weird snow and ice formations inside the crater.

The Africa trip was a wonderful experience, yet I had to have my arm twisted to make me go.

CHAPTER TWENTY-SEVEN

A LIFE IN TRANSITION

During the 1970s and 1980s, I continued to receive honorary degrees—from the University of Massachusetts in 1972, Boston College in 1974, Harvard in 1975, Babson College in 1980, and Curry College in 1982.

I'll never forget the presentation at Boston College. I was on the dais and a large area on the football field was filled with people. I was just about to be given my degree when a streaker ran across the playing field. The president of the college had a wonderful sense of humor, and said, "I guess that nothing I can say will make you all as happy as what we've just seen."

The Harvard degree was a great surprise to me, and I've always thought that one of our good friends must have coaxed them to do it. Harvard is not an easy place from which to get an honorary degree; you have to do something very special. The best part was the statement included with the degree: "Traveler, explorer and map maker. He has moved mountains by changing a dusty Boston institution into a lively educational adventure for young and old." Somebody must have worked very hard to summarize my life in those few words.

I was no longer climbing mountains, but I was keeping very busy. In the early 1970s I made a new map of the Squam

In September 1970, four decades after climbing Les Gaillants-Chamonix, I was reunited with our famed guide Alfred Adolphe Couttet. I remembered that first ascent of the North Face of the Aiguille Verte (13,770 feet) as by far my best alpine climb.

Range in New Hampshire, the area that had been very dear to me in my youth. The map included the small mountains that lie around Squam Lake; they're about 2,000 feet high and an awful lot of people hike along the trails.

In 1976, I returned to Alaska for three high-altitude flights over Mount McKinley for the Rowland Foundation, and made a pack-train and helicopter trip to complete the control for maps of the Muldrow Glacier. The high-altitude flights reached 41,000 feet (in contrast, when I was shooting photographs of McKinley in the 1930s, we flew at about the altitude of the mountain, 20,000 feet).

Later, we used a modified Learjet. Barbara and I had made a trip to Prudhoe Bay with a friend of ours, Charles Towill (he was the public relations chief for British Petroleum, and we had visited the beginning of the trans-Alaska pipeline). Flying back to Anchorage past Mount McKinley, I looked down at the mountain, where there were two enormous masses of thunderclouds. I said to Barbara, "My God, if we could ever take pictures of what we're seeing now, it would be really thrilling." Suddenly, I had an idea.

I contacted Dr. Edwin Land of Polaroid, and he contributed to the modification of the jet. We installed an emergency door fit with a three-quarter-inch optical glass window. This was forty years after I had flown around McKinley with the door of the plane taken off; now we could work in our shirtsleeves. On September 22, 1978, Barbara joined me on a marvelous twilight flight over Mount McKinley. However, we promptly ran into an unanticipated problem when the window iced over. I thought, "Oh, God, we've spent all this money on the window and it's a flop."

Then I got an idea. There were four of us in the cabin, and our breathing was making the upper part of the cabin very humid. If we put the intake for the window defroster on the floor, the air there wouldn't be humid at all. This worked perfectly. I made a thrilling batch of new Mount McKinley pictures with my huge, fifty-pound Fairchild K-6 camera.

In 1980, I went to Anchorage as a consultant to the Alaska State Parks system, to study the establishment of a large new facility for recreation and tourism on the southwestern approach to Mount McKinley, at the gateway to the Tokositna Valley. I told them the Tokositna was one of the most beautiful

In 1980, as a consultant to the Alaska State Parks system, I recommended the establishment of a large new facility for recreation and tourism on the south-western approach to Mount McKinley, at the gateway to the Tokositna Valley. It never panned out.

views of McKinley, but that it had the liability of being on the south side where the weather is often lousy. I went, gave my recommendations, and they paid no attention to anything I said.

On May 1, 1980, I retired as director of the Museum of Science, after forty-one years on the job. I was seventy years old. The museum gave a dinner in honor of Barbara and me on May 28. That gave me the chance to thank, by name, many of the people who had been so helpful to us over the years. I said in my remarks, "We're here tonight to rejoice in our survival over these forty-one eventful years, but this also gives us a marvelous opportunity to thank you for all of the exciting things that you've done. After all, if you hadn't done so much, none of us would be here to rejoice about anything. Every single one of you has played an important part in our lives, and in the life of this museum.

"Mel Payne of the National Geographic Society recently asked me what I felt had been at the focus of my life. The answer I gave could equally apply to this museum: A fascination for discovery. A love of high and distant places. The joy of sharing natural beauty and scientific information with others."

I retired as director with a sense of pride and accomplishment—but I didn't leave the museum. I became chairman of the corporation, then Founding Director, and I maintained an office there for about twenty more years. And soon after I retired as director, I began working on the mapping of Mount Everest. I was too old to climb it, but I was thrilled to become involved with the tallest mountain in the world in a different way.

A great blizzard stacked up the snow outside our Belmont, Massachusetts, home in February 1978.

Chapter Twenty-Eight

Mapping Mount Everest and Keeping Barbara Alive

In the fall of 1981, I was invited by the Chinese Academy of Science to lecture on my experiences mapping Mount McKinley and the Grand Canyon. The trip involved studying the cartography of the Himalaya, and was the first step in winning permission from the governments of China and Nepal to map Everest. We wanted approval for a high-altitude photo flight across part of Tibet to make a new, large-scale map of Everest for the National Geographic Society.

Barbara and I left Hong Kong in early November for the first leg of our flights across China. Our baggage was very carefully examined before we took the big step into China. However, when we arrived in Canton, we couldn't find Barbara's passport. After a frantic search, I left Barbara at the airport (between two armed guards), and rushed to the U.S. Consul to try to get her a new passport. When he heard the story, he was horrified, and said that it would take at least two days. Barbara needed to have three pictures taken, and obtain proof of U.S. citizenship. To the consul's amazement, I reached into my briefcase and gave him a half-dozen excellent pictures of Barbara, as well as a birth certificate. In next to no time, I returned to the airport with all this data, and her guards promptly released her.

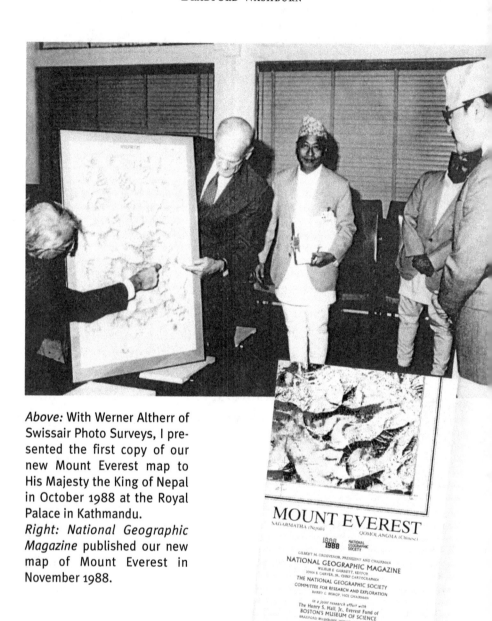

Above: With Werner Altherr of Swissair Photo Surveys, I presented the first copy of our new Mount Everest map to His Majesty the King of Nepal in October 1988 at the Royal Palace in Kathmandu.

Right: National Geographic Magazine published our new map of Mount Everest in November 1988.

We spent a night in Canton, then headed to the airport for the 850-mile flight to Xian, where we waited for a couple of hours before our 300-mile afternoon flight to Lanzhou. There were three inches of snow on the ground and the Xian terminal was frigid. While walking back and forth in an effort to keep warm, we ran into another couple doing exactly the same thing. It turned out to be the new naval attaché of the U.S. consulate in Hong Kong, making a trip around China to become familiar with all the other U.S. consuls in the country. They urged us to have dinner with them in Hong Kong at the end of our trip.

In Lanzhou, we were met by a huge, jolly fellow named Wang Wenying, who was to drive us to our hotel. Wang, who became a lifelong friend, showed us several memorable days in Lanzhou. On the second day, we were brought to a large room, on the walls of which were at least two dozen excellent Chinese maps of Tibet. The most interesting one was a remarkable and detailed map of Mount Everest, which the Tibetans called Chomolungma, the Goddess Mother of the Earth. Since they always looked southward at Everest, the top of the map pointed south, instead of north.

Although the Chinese insisted that detailed aerial photographs had not been used to make this map, it was obvious that they had been. There were dozens of small maps of the northern edge of the Himalaya in their display. I asked why they had such an interest in the many tiny glaciers shown in these maps. Their amazing answer was that the government was studying the possibility of industrializing Tibet, and those glaciers would be the only source of water if they did so.

At the end of our visit, Barbara and I were told that we could bring home any one of the maps they had proudly showed us. I selected the wonderful Everest map, only to be told that it was the only one we couldn't have. Two days later, we headed for Peking (now Bejing), and Wang drove us to the airport. When Barbara went to the ladies room, Wang gave me a bundle of Chinese newspapers to read during our seven-hundred-mile flight, knowing very well that I couldn't understand a word of Chinese. However, carefully buried inside that package was the secret map of Everest! It now resides in the archives of the National Geographic Society in Washington.

While in Peking, we had several wonderful dinners with distinguished Chinese professors whom I had met in 1948 (during the awful experience in Shanghai and Nanking with Milton Reynolds). On November 20 we received permission from the People's Republic of China to extend our mapping twenty-five miles into Tibet. The Chinese government was not particularly interested in what we were doing, but they were not opposed to it.

On the evening before our long, nonstop flight from Peking to Hong Kong, we had dinner with an old friend, Professor Yadunath Khanal of Nepal, who had become the Nepalese ambassador to China. At the close of dinner, he said that the government of Nepal had granted permission for us to fly over Everest (or Sagarmatha, as the Nepalese called it). When I asked Khanal how he had gotten permission, he simply said, "Don't ask. Don't worry. You've got it."

The next morning, we flew on to Hong Kong and I telephoned our attaché friends at the U.S. Consulate to see if they still wanted us to have dinner. They answered with a resounding yes—we had forgotten it was Thanksgiving Day. When I gave the news to Barbara, I said that I had to get my pants cleaned. I had been eating with chopsticks for weeks, and they were filthy. When I took them off for cleaning, what did I find in my hip pocket? Barbara's passport! I had been sitting on it throughout our entire trip, without noticing it.

That was the beginning of the Everest mapping project. It turned out that more permission was indeed needed from the Nepalese government, however. The negotiations went on through 1983, and the final approval for the flights funded by the National Geographic Society was not given until February of 1984. There must have been seventeen or eighteen versions of the damned agreement before everybody finally signed—it was just plain diplomatic constipation.

The National Geographic gave us the grants to carry out the flights over 380 square miles of Nepal and Tibet. By this time I had been appointed a consultant to Swissair Photo Surveys in connection with the project. Our main contact in China was Jun Yong Chen, the senior advisor to the National Bureau of Surveying and Mapping in Peking.

We planned to make our first flights in December of 1984, because we had to take the vertical pictures of the peaks below us when the mountain was entirely free of storms, in flawless weather. Don't ever try to do anything in Nepal between June and September, the monsoon season.

Though the Nepalese couldn't understand why we wanted to map all that uninhabited snow and ice, they were very nice to us. The surveyor general of Nepal, Buddhi Narayan Shrestha, was a helluva good guy. And Bob Bates, my old classmate and climbing friend, had been head of the Peace Corps in Nepal, which helped me to get a foothold in Nepal.

We flew from Boston to Nepal on November 24. I brought my big Fairchild camera, and we planned to use a Learjet. We had two hundred rolls of superb Aerocolor-2445 film, which was identical to the film I had a tested through the window of the jet over McKinley. National Geographic sent Barry Bishop, one of the first Americans to climb Everest in 1963, to handle the administration and the politics (he had a

Ph.D. in Nepalese studies). Werner Altherr of Swissair arrived to take charge of the two flights. We were going to make these flights in late December, but the timing depended entirely on the weather. One flight was for vertical mapping photography, and the second was just for beautiful pictures. The mapping pictures had to be made at an altitude of exactly 39,000 feet—10,000 feet above the top of Mount Everest. The beautiful photographs could be taken at any altitude, primarily with Everest towering above us.

But all our plans began to fall apart soon after we arrived in Katmandu. After dinner one night, Barbara had a temperature of 100 degrees. Then her temperature soared up to 103. I was giving her aspirin, and I knew that if her temperature got much above 104, she could have brain damage. We got a Nepalese doctor in to see her, to try to find out what was wrong, without success.

There was a health center in Katmandu run by westerners, and they couldn't figure out what the hell was wrong with her, either. There are three or four illnesses that almost everyone in that part of the world gets, and they treated Barbara for all of them, expecting her to get well immediately. But none of the medication worked. Then the doctors threw in the towel. They said, "You had better get her to Bangkok, where the doctors and hospital are better."

Four or five days had passed, and I was alarmed. We flew to Bangkok and got her into the Bangkok Nursing Home, an excellent, modern hospital, and Barbara was there for two or three days without improvement. One night, about 9:00 P.M., the doctor in charge called me in my room, and said he wanted to see me the next morning. When I asked why, he said that things were rather complicated. "Well, anything you can tell me tomorrow morning you can tell me right now on the telephone," I replied. And he said, "Your wife is dying of cancer and she is going to die within a week, and, if you don't get her out of here immediately, she's going to die here. If you want her to die at home, you'd better get out of here in a hurry."

That doctor scared the hell out of me. I believed the doctor, and my only thought was getting us onto the next flight to Europe. It was lucky that I was working with Swissair. Miraculously, there were two empty seats on a DC-10 flying to Zurich that night. We flew all night, and landed in a blinding snowstorm. (In fact, when our wheels hit the ground I thought we were still flying, it was snowing so hard.) They put Barbara in a little room at the airport, and in the afternoon we flew first class to Boston. Our daughter Betsy met us at the airport, and we zoomed right off to Massachusetts General, one of the top hospitals in the world. Even there, they couldn't figure out what was wrong with Barbara.

The doctors took a lot of X-rays, and said that they didn't look good at all; they said, "Obviously, she's dying, and if we can't do something pretty damned fast, she's going to be dead." Then, one of the doctors said, "You know, in my second year of medical school I learned about a disease that had most of Barbara's symptoms. It's called Wegener's granulomatosis." He ran the test, and indeed she had Wegener's disease. They gave her cytoxan and prednisone, and her temperature went right down to normal. She owed her life to this terrific young doctor, because she would have been dead in another three or four days if he hadn't found out what was wrong. Years later, we returned to the hospital in Bangkok. When we saw the doctor again, he burst into tears and said, "I made a bad diagnosis." I said, "Brother, that was the most important diagnosis of Barbara's life. Because you made a mistake, we got home."

Meanwhile, back in Nepal, my flights were scheduled to go off—and they did, on December 20 and 22, without me. I had full confidence in Barry Bishop and Werner, and Bill Thompson, a *National Geographic* photographer, was there to take the high-altitude pictures. But Bill didn't get the big, color obliques that I would have gotten if I had been there. For me, that was an absolute disaster, because I knew we could never repeat the ordeal of getting permission. Bill had never used the big camera before, and he was scared of it, so he took all his pictures in 35 millimeter. They were superb, but paled in comparison to what we would have gotten if he had used my big camera. And he didn't know anything about the area, so he couldn't direct the pilot to the most exciting photo opportunities.

The Everest map was published by the National Geographic Society in 1988, and circulated to 10.6 million of its members. The Swiss would have loved to print the map, but they couldn't print 10 million of anything, so the printing job was given to an outfit named Meeham-Tookier in the New Jersey Meadowlands area, right near the football stadium. They printed something like twenty thousand maps an hour, using six tank cars full of ink, and six thousand miles of paper. Werner came from Switzerland, and he and I sat and watched the whole printing process.

As a thank you, we returned to Nepal to present the first copy of our new Mount Everest map to the king and prime minister in a private audience. Then we delivered the second copy to China, at their Academy of Science. The Chinese didn't seem to care very much, but the Nepalese were very happy to see it.

Chapter Twenty-Nine

Everest's Secrets

The mystery of George Mallory and Sandy Irvine's disappearance on Everest in 1924 has fascinated me for most of my life—ever since I heard Capt. John Noel at Groton in 1926, and then met Noel Odell, the last person to see them alive, at Harvard a few years later.

Odell and I had both agreed that when he last saw Mallory and Irvine, they had arrived at the top of what we call the "first step" on Everest's ridge. If you continue up that ridge—which they did, because he saw them go on, before they disappeared into the afternoon clouds—you run into the "second step." Nobody has ever climbed that second step. It's a tremendous cliff; if you run into it, you can't go around to the left at all. You can't go straight up it because it's absolutely vertical. I don't know whether it's minus handholds, but I know that nobody has ever climbed it.

Everyone who has gotten past the second step has gone down to the right of it, passed it a bit, and then gone straight up a crack behind it. The Chinese were the first to climb it this way, years and years ago. They left an aluminum ladder there to make it easier for others to get through; but without that ladder, it would be very difficult climbing.

I think that Mallory and Irvine reached that point on the ridge. They had gotten a late start, and it was late in the afternoon. It was perfectly clear to both of them that they weren't going to get to the top, which was still several hundred feet above them. They started back to camp, and how they got lost is anybody's guess. It wasn't a bad night at all—Odell told me that there were only a few fair-weather clouds, and that there was no storm.

I'm sure they were in the clouds; when they went down the ridge (with camp being just off the crest of the ridge), did they cut off to the left too soon, and go further and further down? Irvine, who was younger and inexperienced, was Mallory's partner for two reasons. The first was that Mallory liked him; and the second was that Mallory was a nut on oxygen, which in those days came in extremely awkward and very heavy bottles. Sandy Irvine liked to play around with tools, and helped Mallory keep his oxygen equipment running properly. One of those bottles was found way up on the ridge a few years ago.

So they headed back to camp, and they turned off that ridge too soon. They kept going in the clouds, and then it became dark, and I think Irvine slipped or tripped in the darkness, and yanked Mallory off his feet, and Mallory hit his head on the only sizeable sharp rock on that whole slope. The slope is essentially composed of ledges, forty degrees, which is not steep. There are almost no vertical places you could fall down, but Mallory slipped. I choose to believe he was yanked off his feet by Sandy Irvine, and where he came down, he hit his head on a big, sharp rock. He survived that fall, albeit briefly, because when his body was found, he was grasping: his fingers were frozen in that position, trying to stop himself from sliding.

Now, I'm the only person who has ever suggested what might have happened if he hadn't been hurt. That is what's most interesting to me. In 2001, Eric Simonson led the investigative expedition that found Mallory's body, and they took extraordinary pictures, so we know exactly where he died.

I've studied the climb, and I know the configuration of Everest extremely well from our very detailed mapping. Mallory was way to the left of where he thought he was, sixty degrees to the left of their camp. If they had gone another five hundred feet in the direction in which they seemed to be going, they would have gone over a cliff. Assuming this was in the dark, they'd probably both have been killed, and they would have plain disappeared. They did disappear for a helluva long time.

One wonders if Irvine's body will be found someday. Sandy Irvine had a Kodak camera that was the exactly the same as the one I used in the Alps, at more or less the same time. Irvine's camera is one of the most famous in the world, because people wonder if he took pictures of them reaching the summit. Many are certain that if Irvine's body is ever found it will be way up on the mountain with the camera in his pocket. And because it's so cold up there year-round, the chances are very good that any film would still reveal something about what was going on (unless the camera had been inside his clothing and heated up, and thawed the film).

I think Irvine was hitched to Mallory, and the rope was thrashing around, and the chances are more than fifty-fifty that when he became detached from Mallory, he just slipped down the slope and was blown away. I hope that his body is found, with his camera, because if the film is developed, I know it's not going to show that they made the summit. There isn't a snowball's chance in hell that they got anywhere near the top. There was a helluva a lot of climbing yet to do above the spot where Mallory was found.

Everest is the highest mountain in the world, so people are always going to be interested in what happened there—and interested in its precise altitude. In May 1992, working with a young expert from the Nepalese survey department, and with the help of American mountaineers, we made the first laser measurement of the top of Everest: 29,028 feet. Vernon Tejas, the Alaskan mountaineering guide who was the first man to complete a solo winter ascent of Mount McKinley, took prisms up and planted them on Everest's summit. One of the most exciting moments in my life was looking through the telescope, from a hill above downtown Namche, and seeing the brilliant ruby laser reflections dancing on the top of Everest. That was the beginning of my effort to get at the true altitude of the peak.

When I was kid, Everest was considered to be 29,002 feet high. The British surveyor George Everest, for whom the mountain is named, and his successors, established the 29,002-foot altitude way back during the survey of India. He marked six places and divided them to get an average. As I said, we measured it at 29,028 feet in 1992. A few years later, I pushed for another remeasurement of Everest. Exciting new equipment was available that could obtain a more precise measurement of the height. I was certain there would be a small change. In 1999, the Mount Everest Research Expedition was undertaken by the National Geographic Society and Boston's Museum of Science to remeasure the mountain. Pete Athans (who has climbed Everest six times—more than any other American) and Sherpa Chewang Nima brought a Trimble 4800 GPS unit to the summit on May 5, 1999, and ran it for several minutes on a cloudless, windless day. The Trimble measured the altitude of Everest by Global Positioning Satellites. Without Pete we wouldn't have gotten that new altitude for Everest. The Chinese, under my friend, Dr. J. Y. Chen, performed measurements. The U.S. Geodetic Survey came up with their own number, as did Dr. David Mencin. The average of these new calculations was 8,850 meters, or 29,035 feet.

One hundred or two hundred years from now, I'm sure that Everest will be a little taller. The Alps were originally formed over what is now Africa, and shoved up on top of Europe. They are wearing out, basically wearing down. The Himalaya are in just the opposite situation: India is being shoved under China by tectonic plates and that is constantly forcing the mountain upward. So the chances are that Everest's altitude will increase. In addition, all of us—and especially Roger Bilham, a scientific expert on plate tectonics—believe that whenever there is an earthquake in the region (and there will be one), Everest will go up slightly.

Some years before the newest measurements were recorded, I had the opportunity to spend time with another major figure from Everest history, Sir John Hunt. John Hunt was the leader of the expedition that put Sir Edmund Hillary and Tenzing Norgay on the top of the world, and he wrote the book about the expedition's success. His efforts were overshadowed by the achievement of Hillary and Tenzing, but the expedition couldn't have come off without his leadership. Together we were honored in Switzerland in 1994, receiving the first King Albert Gold Medals for Outstanding Achievement in the Mountain World.

For the presentation ceremony, they took us outside of Zurich to an old monastery. The fellow reading the citations was on the other side of a beautiful, ancient rug, and told us that we had to take our shoes off and walk across the rug in our stocking feet. John Hunt leaned over to Barbara and said,

"I have a hole in my stocking." He took off his shoes, anyway, and his toe was sticking out during this serious ceremony.

In 2003, there were celebrations around the world for the fiftieth anniversary of that first ascent by Hillary and Tenzing. Ed Hillary has behaved superbly with the fame he gained from Everest, right from the beginning. He has donated a great deal of money to the Nepalese, to build schools and hospitals for youngsters; everybody in Nepal just crosses themselves when they talk about Ed Hillary. They love him.

It seemed petty to me when people asked which of them had made it to the summit first. Hillary and Tenzing were both on the same snowdrift. The pictures indicate that they climbed over a thousand vertical feet that day (more than anybody who climbs Everest does today, because of the way the route has changed). They also had the highest camp, in a miserable place, open to the weather. There was nothing easy about what Hillary and Tenzing did.

I remember exactly where I was when I heard that Everest had been climbed for the first time. I was in my auto, driving myself over to my office at Harvard's Geographical Institute. That was a thrilling moment you can't duplicate.

I have spent a lot of time working on Everest in recent years. I enjoy talking to climbers about Mallory. I like the technical aspects of it. And I met Hillary about ten years ago. Every so often I come across something interesting about Everest and send it to him. At my age, it's interesting to still be working on a project that doesn't have a definite answer. It gives you something to point for, something new to try to find.

CHAPTER THIRTY

DINING WITH PRESIDENTS AND OTHER HONORS

I met Franklin Delano Roosevelt when he was president, because his son, Elliott, was in my class at Groton. During my World War II service on the cold-weather testing project, we worked through FDR, but I never saw him then. And then I knew Jack Kennedy from Massachusetts, but before he became president. He was a trustee of the Museum of Science for a while.

In December of 1983, Barbara and I were guests at a state dinner at the White House, given by President and Mrs. Ronald Reagan to honor the king and queen of Nepal. When we met Nancy Reagan, I told her that I had known her step-father Loyal Davis. She looked at me and said, "I know all about that." And that was the end of that conversation, just like snapping your fingers.

President Reagan was an absolutely fabulous speaker. He said he had never had such a wonderful day as that day with his majesty from Nepal. "Everything we discussed, we agreed upon," he said, "and I wish I could spend a day like that with Tip O'Neill." (O'Neill, of course, was the speaker of the House and a Democrat.) And it brought the house down.

The Republican Party of Massachusetts held a big event at the museum, just before my retirement as director in 1980. We

Here we are, triumphant, atop 10,000-foot Mount Bertha on the first ascent, July 30, 1940. In November 1980, the same year we were presented with the first Alexander Graham Bell Medal by the National Geographic Society, they unveiled a painting by William Draper based on this photo by Tom Winship. The painting now hangs in the lobby of the Boston Museum of Science.

met President Gerald Ford at that time. Barbara and I had a special gift made up for him—a plastic block with a chunk of rock from the very top of Mount McKinley, and pieces from the bottom of the Grand Canyon and Badwater in Death Valley, the lowest point in the United States. However, the gift was not ready in time for the event and it was apparently misplaced. Twelve years later, in the spring of 1992, the gift turned up and I mailed it to Ford in California, where he had retired. Some months later I got a thank-you note from the former president. He apologized for the delay in replying, noting that he had been laid up in the hospital from a knee joint replacement operation when it arrived, and then he had been busy campaigning for the first George Bush. He said he had put the artifact on display in his office.

In the nearly twenty-five years since my retirement from the museum, Barbara and I have received many honors:

In November 1980, we were presented with the first Alexander Graham Bell Medal by the National Geographic Society, "for unique and notable contributions to the science of geography through exploration and discovery over more than four decades and culminating in the first large-scale map of the heart of the Grand Canyon of the Colorado."

In 1988, as part of the one hundredth anniversary of the National Geographic Society, we were honored with a Centennial Award—a globe of the world, made of Steuben glass, a gorgeous thing we keep in our living room. The award cited illustrious careers in mountaineering, exploring, mapping, and museum administration, and the inscription read: "The Washburns symbolized the great traditions of the Society's earliest explorers of geographic and cultural frontiers." It was a very special award, and among the small number of other people honored were Sir Edmund Hillary, Dr.

Mary Leakey and Richard Leakey, Senator John Glenn, Jane Goodall, and Jacques-Yves Cousteau. What an unforgettable experience! You can't beat it. It summed up my life's work.

In 1995, Barbara was presented an honorary degree from the University of Alaska. It was a Doctor of Science degree. I got a big kick out of it—a wonderful event, with so many people attending, and Barbara as the focus of attention. That made for two doctors in the family, but I haven't addressed her as Dr. Washburn.

In May 1997, the Alaska Legislature passed a resolution praising Barbara and me that read, "Come now the Twentieth Alaska Legislature to recognize, salute, and thank Bradford and Barbara Polk Washburn for their many achievements in the arts and for their contributions to the sum of the world's knowledge. While many Alaskans know the Washburns for their explorations and photos of Mount McKinley, the arts and sciences celebrate the Washburns' fame not only as photographers, but also as mountaineers, geographers, cartographers, authors and innovators."

In October 2001, we jointly received the Lowell Thomas Award of the Explorer's Club, along with Edmund Hillary and distinguished mountaineer Ed Viesturs. Some years before that I had received the Explorers Medal, the highest honor of the Explorers Club in New York.

And in January, 2003, *Climbing* magazine gave me its "Lifetime Achievement Award."

I can't help but reflect on the role of exploration in modern society, when it seems as if all of the frontiers of the earth have been studied.

Current explorations must extend beyond the earth's boundaries. They use the Hubbell Telescope to look millions of miles away; maybe if I had come along later, that's what I would have worked on. Pictures taken through telescopes are sharp when they're moving at 18,000 mph to stay in orbit. And we can see them with crystal clarity.

In 1935, when we took our trip to explore the Yukon, nobody else had ever been there. No one had even taken an airplane into that territory. My generation was lucky to have frontiers that we could reach and explore, and maps that we could produce to explain what we had found. That's quite different from going into space, or looking into space, where there isn't any end at all.

At eighty-eight years of age, I won a dare when, at the dedication of Milton Academy's new climbing wall on February 22, 1999, somebody challenged me to climb it. I made it to the top without trouble.

CHAPTER THIRTY-ONE

IT'S A WONDERFUL LIFE

In 1988, I published a map of Mount Washington that I worked on with my friend Casey Hodgdon. The mapmaking required hiking over old trails, and it was great fun. We got vertical photography of the trail in the fall when the leaves were off the trees. That made it easy to find the trails above timberline; the footpaths and brooks were visible.

We used a three-hundred-foot tape for measuring, and took turns walking from the tape to the brook. Then we sketched what was in between. Once, I tripped and fell flat on my face, where I discovered a piece of wire. I said, "What the hell is this?" and followed the wire for a couple hundred yards to the remains of a lumber camp that was a century old.

Casey and I ended up walking hundreds of miles. Barbara joined us for some of it, and we had other volunteers helping; but Casey and I did the majority of the work. Most of the detail work on that map was done with a helicopter, or by driving up Mount Washington and then hiking down. Given how often I climbed Mount Washington, it is ironic that I did not climb it while making the map. (You can make a map just as easily by going downhill as you can by going up.)

If someone asked how I've managed to stay so vigorous

into my nineties, I would say I didn't take good care of myself, but apparently the way I lived was good enough. Normal sleep. Not eating heavily. Not much liquor, and no smoking. Barbara is always after me, saying that we've got to get out and walk more. I've never been interested in walking to walk. I've walked like hell going somewhere, but I have not necessarily been interested in it just to make a pointless lap.

We've both been lucky to maintain our health well enough to travel often, although in 1991, I had triple heart-bypass surgery. I was feeling fine, but my doctor said, "You know, at your age, you really ought to have a stress test." I ran on a treadmill that sped faster and grew steeper, and in short order, they took me off the machine, put me on a stretcher, and drove directly to Massachusetts General. The doctors identified a blockage and suggested I come back in six months for an operation. I figured I might have a heart attack in the meanwhile, so I suggested that since I was all prepped for it, they should just do it now. They had an opening (I guess another patient died), and surgery was scheduled the next morning. My recovery took about a month. Afterward, I didn't realize how weak I was until I walked down the front steps. It was quite a job to get back to the front door.

In February 1999, a climbing wall about thirty feet tall was built in memory of my old friend Ad Carter at Milton Academy. I was there for the opening; I was eighty-eight years old, and they dared me to try it. Much to my surprise, I still had a lot of strength in my fingers. I went all the way to the top. There's this funny picture of me on the climbing wall wearing a dress shirt and tie. When I started up, I didn't have the slightest idea what would happen. I got to the top, and there was a rope. I announced, "Well, here I am. I've made it. I'm going to jump off now." And I jumped—and they let me down with a pulley.

In 2001, on the occasion of my seventy-fifth anniversary as a member, the Appalachian Mountain Club gave me a lifetime achievement award. They cited my first climb of Mount Washington in 1921, and the map of Mount Washington and the Presidential Range.

After all of these years, I still try to visit Mount Washington every year. I'm too old to climb it now, but usually, in midsummer, Barbara and I drive up the auto road to the top of the mountain. I love it. As soon as we get above timberline, the views are marvelous. (I do miss walking in the hills of the Presidential Range.)

It's very nice to be recognized. But I didn't climb mountains in Alaska or make maps to be recognized. I did them because I wanted to. There were a lot of firsts, but doing things first isn't always the best thing. I know people who have said how tragic it must have been to be the guy, Roger Bannister, who first ran the four-minute mile. What did he do after that? Once a barrier is broken, you can't do much more. In some ways, breaking the four-minute mile is like being the first person to stand on top of Mount Everest. Then people say, "What is there that can be done to take the next step?" And there isn't a next step.

I was lucky to live when I did, when there were so many things no one had done before.

I've had a wonderful life, working with, and for, so many interesting people, many of them from the National Geographic Society. If it hadn't been for them, none of the big maps would have been made. National Geographic funded the early maps and, in recent years, the museum's Robert Dunn fund gave me financial help in writing and illustrating books and articles on exploration.

When I consider all of my climbs in Alaska, there is no doubt that the Lucania trip was the one that gave me the greatest satisfaction—climbing Lucania was almost a religious experience. Of course, I am best known in Alaska for my association with Mount McKinley. I am best known in Boston for my work with the Museum of Science. I am best known other places for my photography, or for making my maps. I suppose I could make the argument that when I die, I would like to be remembered simply as somebody who liked to do things well.

I would have loved to have climbed Everest. Other than that, I don't have any regrets in life. I am gratified and happy. We had three neat kids and nine grandchildren. The museum, which was my lifetime job, is a great success. And I am very lucky that I had a marriage with Barbara that is still going strong after sixty-four years. That is clearly the best thing of all.

Throughout most of my career, I have kept close to my heart this passage from "The Explorer," written by Rudyard Kipling in 1898:

"Something hidden. Go and find it. Go and look behind the Ranges. Something lost behind the Ranges. Lost and waiting for you—Go!"

Taken by David Ochsner in early October 1971, this photo is titled *"Mapping the North Kaibab Trail of the Grand Canyon."*

AFTERWORD

Given the nature of his inquisitive mind, his unflagging energy, and willingness to take on projects when another man his
age would have chosen a life of leisure in the armchair in front
of the television set, it seemed as if Bradford Washburn would
live forever.

Certainly, he packed more than one lifetime's worth of
action and activity into his ninety-six years before he passed
away from heart failure at the retirement home he lived at in
Lexington, Massachusetts, on January 10, 2007.

Although he was a man whose scientific explorations,
work as a cartographer, expeditions as a mountain climber,
and pioneering efforts as a mountain photographer led him to
travels around the world, in another way Washburn never ven-
tured very far from home. He was born and grew up in the
Boston area, maintained his year-round residence in the
immediate area, and maintained a connection to the Boston
Museum of Science from 1939 until his death.

A meticulous planner as an adventurer, Washburn per-
petuated the trait of supreme organization in other aspects of
his life, as well. Even in his last years he had stacks of paperwork
in arranged piles and spread throughout the home he and his
wife of sixty-seven years shared. He always wanted to be able to
put his hands on his papers, whether they were diaries of trips
taken long ago, photographs from trips dating back decades, or
letters seeking his advice about some new way to approach
Mount McKinley.

From the 1940s on, when he climbed McKinley's
20,320-foot peak during World War II, returned in 1947 with

wife, Barbara, who made the first ascent by a woman of the tallest mountain on the North American continent, and led the 1951 assault of the West Buttress route that has become the most popular way up the mountain, Washburn's name has been synonymous with the peak.

To the average man on the street it may not be a sexy accomplishment, but Washburn is also admired in scientific and mountaineering circles as the man who mapped McKinley.

Over the years of my friendship with Brad Washburn I merely had to mention the words "Mount McKinley" and he almost instantly came up with a fresh story to tell, either about one of his own adventures, his ideas for how the climbing season should be administered, or his thoughts about someone else's adventures on the peak.

Washburn was a multifaceted man with many interests, but he understood how closely identified he had become with McKinley and he seemed to relish the chance to talk about the mountain when anyone showed an interest in it.

Many years before his heart gave out on him Washburn had heart surgery and from then on he often made gallows humor jokes about the likelihood of him keeling over suddenly and perishing. Yet he seemed to retain remarkable stamina well into his nineties. It was only the last year or so of his life that Washburn seemed to run short of energy and spent more time at his Lexington home.

When Washburn died he was survived by his three children, Elizabeth (Betsy), Dorothy, and Edward (Teddy), and Barbara, who in November of 2012 celebrated her ninety-eighth birthday.

In 2008, the Bradford Washburn American Mountaineering Museum opened in Golden, Colorado. Its "vision" statement reads in part: "The mission of the Bradford

Washburn American Mountaineering Museum is to inspire in our visitors a greater appreciation of the mountains and for mountaineering, in all its facets, including the cultural and inspirational qualities of the mountains and the sport; to help in the cause to preserve the mountains and the history of mountaineering; to educate our visitors and in so doing enhance their enjoyment and safety in the mountains."

Beginning in 2010, the museum began honoring individuals in its Hall of Mountaineering Excellence, essentially a mountaineering Hall of Fame.

In late autumn of 2009 it was announced that Bradford Washburn would be inducted into the Alaska Sports Hall of Fame. While that young Hall of Fame recognizes athletes in the popular team sports, it also pays homage to those who excel in activities that are appreciated in the Far North, from dog sledding to mountaineering.

On February 25, 2010, Washburn was posthumously inducted into the Alaska Sports Hall of Fame. Barbara did not feel capable of making the four-thousand-mile-plus journey and Washburn was represented by his daughter, Elizabeth Cabot, of Belmont, Massachusetts. During her acceptance speech she said that her dad would have been honored and grateful to be selected.

It was always my theory that the people Washburn hung out with most of the time in Massachusetts knew little about what he was doing when he was off in Alaska during all of those summers since the 1930s. I also thought that the people he was friendly with, climbed with, and spent time with in Alaska on his expeditions probably had little idea of what he was doing in Massachusetts when he was busy running the Boston Museum of Science.

Washburn even teased me that depending on which newspaper was filing his obituary it would lead with completely different facts. In Alaska, he would be exalted for his exploits on McKinley and for climbing other mountains in the state. In Massachusetts, and in the rest of the Lower 48, his work with the museum would be highlighted.

In a remarkable and varied career, he mapped McKinley, Mount Everest, and the Grand Canyon; took photographs while hanging out the doors of low-flying planes; made first ascents of remote Alaska mountains; and created a science museum from scratch. Washburn also wrote books. I chuckled when I realized that some day a reader who was not thoroughly familiar with Washburn's decades of accomplishment would stumble across a list of his works and the dates they were published. Brad wrote boys books in the late 1920s and more than seventy years later he and I collaborated on this volume. I'm assuming that innocent reader will think that the authors were different people, that there must have been a Bradford Washburn writing, then a Bradford Washburn Jr., and then a Bradford Washburn III, and that the bibliography merely omitted the suffixes.

Nope. They were all Brad.

During the summer of 2012, I was in Alaska and stopped in at the Anchorage Museum of History and Art. A featured temporary exhibition included many of Washburn's iconic black-and-white photographs from Mount McKinley. Naturally. Any pictorial documentation of the peak would have been sorely lacking without Brad Washburn pictures. I recognized many of them and it felt good to see them again.

It seems a bit surreal that more than six years have passed since Brad died. I still half expect him to call me to ask when I am coming to Boston again because he's got something to show me. A new format for an old photograph, perhaps, or some writings about a project incubating.

Bradford Washburn was one-of-a-kind. He will be remembered in different circles for different achievements, but he was most proud of building that museum in Boston from a hole in the wall into a modern interactive museum where every school in the metropolitan area takes their elementary school classes to be introduced to science.

They have been doing that for ages in the Boston area. More than fifty years have passed since I was one of those kids who went on such a field trip, long before I knew who Bradford Washburn was.

It would be decades before we met, but those many years later I returned to the museum over and over again to meet with him in the office he kept as long as he was able. There we were in the building I first saw as a child, in the building he built through vigorous fund-raising as a young professional.

Yet I always took a quiet, pleasant satisfaction in seeing a Bradford Washburn photograph of Mount McKinley hanging on the wall in that office in Massachusetts. Alaska may have been many miles distant, but it was still close to his heart.

—Lew Freedman
January 2013

MAPS BY BRADFORD WASHBURN

Date Printed	Title
1924	Squam Lake, New Hampshire A boy's chart; only one copy exists
1934	Mount Crillon, Alaska Published in *The Geographical Journal*, London
1936	St. Elias Range, Alaska/Yukon Territory Reconnaissance map for the National Geographic Society
1936-79	Squam Lake Chart #1 (1:15,000) Four editions: 1936, 1948, 1954, 1961
1937	Town of Carlisle, Massachusetts Photo mosaic
1960	Mount McKinley (1:50,000) Swiss Foundation for Alpine Research
1961	Squam Lake Photo mosaic
1968	Mounts Kennedy, Alverstone, and Hubbard (1:31,560) National Geographic Society
1973	Squam Range, New Hampshire (1:15,000)
1974	Inner Canyon, Grand Canyon (1:24,000)
1978	Heart of the Grand Canyon (1:24,000) National Geographic Society
1979	Squam Lake Chart #2 (1:12,500) Several editions
1980	Wonder Lake – McGonagall Pass – Muldrow Glacier (1:24,000)
1981	Bright Angel Trail, Grand Canyon (1:24,000)
1983	Muldrow Glacier Research Maps (5 sheets @ 1:10,000) Swiss Foundation for Alpine Research

1988	Presidential Range, New Hampshire (1:20,000)
1988	Mount Everest (1:50,000) National Geographic Society; an edition of 11 million maps printed and circulated worldwide
1990	Mount Everest Relief Model (1:2500; 2 feet = 1 mile) Contour interval: 15 feet (5 meters) Gift of Henry Hall, made by Rauda Scale Models, Seattle
1991	Mount Everest (1:50,000) Swissphoto Surveys' new edition with climbing statistics on back
1992	Mount Everest's Northwest Face Orthophoto Map (1:5000)
1993	Tuckerman Ravine, New Hampshire (1:5,000) Grand Circle Travel
1998	Mount Everest's South Face & Khumbu Orthophoto Map (1:5,000) Depicts all Southwest ascent routes above Camp 2
2002	Mount Everest above 7,000 Meters (1:5,000) Contour interval: 15 feet (5 meters) Everything from the South Col to the North Col in Tibet

Bradford and Barbara Washburn's Honorary Degrees

1951	Ph.D., University of Alaska
1957	D.Sc., Tufts University
1957	D.Sc., Colby College
1958	D.Sc., Northeastern University
1965	D.F.A., Suffolk University
1972	D.Sc., University of Massachusetts
1974	D.H.L., Boston College
1975	D.H.L., Harvard University
1980	D.Sc., Babson College
1982	D.Sc., Curry College
1996	D.Sc., Boston University *
2001	D.Sc., Simmons College *
2002	D.Sc., Plymouth, New Hampshire State College

* indicates that Mrs. Washburn received this degree at the same ceremony

Bradford and Barbara Washburn's Awards and Prizes

1938   Cuthbert Peek Award, Royal Geographic Society,
        London, England

1940   Burr Prize, for "Outstanding Exploration in Alaska,"
        National Geographic Society

1944   Exceptional Service Award, Commanding General, Alaska

1946   Exceptional Civilian Service Award, U.S. Secretary of War

1957   Gold Medal, Harvard Travelers Club

1965   Burr Prize (for a second time), National Geographic
        Society

1966   Day Medal, Philadelphia Academy of Arts and Sciences

1970   Julius A. Stratton Prize, American Friends of
        Switzerland

1970   Business Statesman Award, Harvard Business
        School Association of Boston

1974   New Englander of the Year, New England Council

1979   Gold Research Medal, to Bradford and Barbara
        Washburn, for "Outstanding Cartographic
        Research," Royal Scottish Geographical Society

1980   Alexander Graham Bell Award, to Bradford and
        Barbara Washburn, the first Bell Award given,
        for "Four decades of exploration and discovery,"
        National Geographic Society

1983   Distinguished Bostonian Award, Boston Chamber of
        Commerce

1984   Explorers Medal, highest award of the Explorers Club

1985   Highest Award, for "Lifelong contributions to
        exploratory surveying and cartography,"
        Engineering Societies of New England.

1988   Centennial Award, to Bradford and Barbara Washburn, for"An illustrious career of mountaineering, exploring, mapping, and museum administration," National Geographic Society

1988   Cherry Kearton Medal, for "Achievement in cartography and photography," Royal Geographic Society

1991   Joe Dodge Award, "In recognition of outstanding service to the public in the White Mountains of New Hampshire, 1921-1991," Appalachian Mountain Club

1994   King Albert Award, of Switzerland, a gold medal for"Outstanding achievement in the mountain world." Given at the same time to Sir John Hunt, leader of the British team (Hillary and Tenzing) that made the first ascent of Mount Everest.

1996   Special Award for "Outstanding contribution to public understanding of geology," American Geological Institute

1997   Commissioner's Award, to Bradford and Barbara Washburn, for "Lasting contributions to the mapping of the St. Elias Range," Government of Canada's Yukon Territory

1997   Certificate of Honor, to Bradford and Barbara Washburn, from the Alaska State Legislature, signed by Speaker of the House of Representatives and the President of the Senate, citing the Washburns as "authors, climbers, and artists who have pursued the impossible dream and made it not only real, but accessible to us all."

1998   Honorary Fellow, Royal Geographical Society, London, England

1998   Installation of world's highest Global Positioning Satellite Station by guide Wally Berg, in the Washburn expedition to Mount Everest. Installed for operation at the South Col, altitude 25,888.501 feet.

1999	The Commonwealth Award, to Bradford and Barbara Washburn, the highest award given to any citizen of the State of Massachusetts, The Massachusetts Cultural Council
2000	Discovery Lifetime Award, to Bradford and Barbara Washburn, for "A lifetime spent in developing our knowledge about the environment, and raising awareness, enthusiasm, and understanding in others about the nature of our world," Royal Geographical Society, Institute of British Geographers, and the Discovery Channel.
2001	Lifetime Achievement Award, Appalachian Mountain Club, February 10, on the occasion of the club's 125th anniversary celebration.
	50th Anniversary Celebration, July 10, marking the date of the Washburn team's first ascent of Mount McKinley's West Buttress, the route by which virtually all mountaineers now reach the summit of the highest peak in North America. Washburn was the last living member of the seven-man team that made that historic climb.
	Lowell Thomas Award, to Bradford and Barbara Washburn, for "Outstanding careers in mountaineering," Explorers Club, on October 29, a celebration that also honored Sir Edmund Hillary and Ed Viesturs.
2003	Lifetime Achievement Award, North American Nature Photographers Association
2008	The Bradford Washburn American Mountaineering Museum opens in Golden, Colorado.
2010	Inducted into the Alaska Sports Hall of Fame, Anchorage, Alaska.

ABOUT THE COAUTHOR

Lew Freedman was a friend of Bradford Washburn for the last two decades of his life and spent considerable time with Washburn in their shared home state of Massachusetts, and in Alaska, where Freedman lived for seventeen years.

They collaborated and cooperated on a number of writing projects, including several stories for the *Anchorage Daily News* and a volume excerpting Washburn's expedition diaries, in addition to this autobiography.

Freedman is the author of nearly sixty books, more than twenty of them about Alaska, and is the winner of more than 250 journalism awards. He lives in Indiana with his wife, Debra.

Printed in the USA
CPSIA information can be obtained
at www.ICGtesting.com
JSHW012019140824
68134JS00033B/2777